D1247696

77225

9
N3
6
982

No place to go : effects of compulsory
relocation on Navajos / Thayer
Scudder, with the assistance of David
F. Aberle ... [et al.]. --
Philadelphia : Institute for the
Study of Human Issues, c1982.
xii, 202 p., [10] p. of plates : ill.
; 22 cm. -- (Monographs in development
anthropology)
   Bibliography: p. 191-194.
   ISBN 0-89727-029-0
   1. Navaho Indians--Land transfers.
2. Indians of North America--Arizona--
Land transfers. 3. Hopi Indians--Land
transfers. 4. Relocation (Housing)--
Arizona. I. Scudder, Thayer.

19 JUN 84   7653112 . OMMMxc   81-6723

No Place To Go

Monographs in Development Anthropology

UNDER THE GENERAL EDITORSHIP OF
David W. Brokensha, Michael M. Horowitz, and Thayer Scudder

Sponsored by the Institute for Development Anthropology

No Place To Go

Effects of Compulsory Relocation on Navajos

Thayer Scudder *with the assistance of*
David F. Aberle
Kenneth Begishe
Elizabeth Colson
Clark Etsitty
Jennie Joe
Jerry Kammer
Mary E. D. Scudder
Jeffrey Serena
Betty Beetso Gilbert Tippeconnie
Roy Walters
John Williamson

A Publication of the
Institute for the Study of Human Issues
Philadelphia

Copyright © 1982 by ISHI,
Institute for the Study of Human Issues
All Rights Reserved
No part of this book may be reproduced in any form or by any electronic
or mechanical means including information storage and retrieval
systems without permission in writing from the publisher, except by a
reviewer who may quote brief passages in a review.

Manufactured in the United States of America

Library of Congress Cataloging in Publication Data
Main entry under title:

No place to go.

   (Monographs in development anthropology)
   Bibliography: p.
   1. Navaho Indians—Land transfers. 2. Indians of North America—
Arizona—Land transfers. 3. Hopi Indians—Land transfers. 4. Reloca-
tion (Housing)—Arizona.
I. Scudder, Thayer. II. Series.
E99.N3N6   979.1'00497   81-6723
ISBN 0-89727-029-0   AACR2

For information, write:

Director of Publications
ISHI
3401 Science Center
Philadelphia, Pennsylvania 19104
U.S.A.

Contents

PETER MACDONALD

Contents

Photographs follow page 84

Figures and Tables

Foreword

PETER MACDONALD
Chairman, Navajo Tribal Council

During the past twenty-five years the Navajo people have been conducting a valiant struggle to preserve their cultural heritage and tribal identity. For over a thousand years the Navajos have lived in the high plateau country that forms part of the modern states of Arizona, New Mexico, and Utah. These ancestral lands have given face and form to the tribal traditions and cultural unity that are so important to the Navajo people.

It is tragic, however, that this special bond between the Navajo people and their sacred lands is rarely recognized by non-Indian Americans. It was tragic in 1863, for example, when Colonel Kit Carson led a cavalry column into what is now northern Arizona, rounded up 8,354 Navajo men, women, and children, burned their crops, slaughtered their livestock, and led the people on a 500-mile forced walk into captivity in what is now eastern New Mexico.

It was also tragic more than a century later, in 1974, when the Congress of the United States ordered the eviction of some 6,000 Navajos from their reservation homelands because of an inter-tribal land dispute with the Hopi Indians. Congress' intervention into this land dispute is perhaps the most tragic of all, since it is clear that the government—while attempting to right the wrongs of the past—has only succeeded in compounding the errors of the last century. It was, after all, restrictive government policies that confined both the Navajo and Hopi tribes to the same reservation lands in an exercise of cultural myopia that refused to recognize the differences in tribal traditions and lifestyles of the two peoples.

Until Congress intervened in this land dispute in 1974, the federal government had long recognized that while both the Navajo and the Hopi shared a legal interest in the nearly two million acres of reservation land in Arizona under dispute, the day-to-day possession and use of this area was almost exclusively Navajo, while the Hopis have continued to follow their ancient ways of living in villages on the table-top mesas scattered in 600,000 acres of land not in dispute inside the disputed area.

During 1979 and the early part of 1980, Congress turned once again to the land-dispute issues, this time attempting to provide substitute land, by authorizing the transfer or purchase of land for resettlement purposes. Unfortunately, Congress, as in earlier times, followed the expediencies of politics rather than taking the time to realize what this relocation order would mean in human terms for the Navajo people and adopting a humane, rather than an expedient, solution.

Although the Navajos were authorized to purchase some additional land with tribal funds, it is clear that a majority of relocatees will have to find new homes, probably in resettlement areas in cities such as Flagstaff and Phoenix. For the typical Navajo relocatee, who has lived all his life in the free and open lands of the Navajo Nation, this banishment to an unfamiliar urban setting, far away from the reservation, constitutes little more than a spiritual death sentence.

The "life estate" concept touted as a cure-all by those who supported the 1980 congressional amendments to Public Law 93-531 is an idea totally foreign to Navajo culture and tradition. For the traditional Navajo family, land is something to be held in trust, to be passed on to the next generation. Elderly relatives are a source of wisdom and family continuity and are to be assisted by younger family members. The life estate, in which old people are to be left alone to die, knowing that they will have nothing to pass on to their children, is viewed by our people as an example of barbarism—not civilization.

The 1980 congressional amendments stand in stark contrast to the Maine Indian Claims settlement, in which the policy of the United States to pay off the Indians' land claims with money, while leaving the white settlers in possession of the land, was strictly adhered to. This double standard of justice—forced relocation of Navajos and no relocation of whites—will not be lost on the people of the Third World, on whom this nation is more and more dependent.

The 1980 amendments also make a bad matter worse by creating a "new land dispute": 1,500,000 acres of land, home to over 13,000 Navajos and sadly underdeveloped, may not be developed at all until the conclusion of lengthy federal litigation crawling through the federal courts.

In order to help non-Indian Americans understand the full impact of this eviction program, the Navajo Tribal Council asked Dr. Thayer Scudder, a world-renowned population relocation expert at the California Institute of Technology, to study the human factors involved. His report, recently re-edited, fully documents the devastating effects that the relocation will have on the Navajo people, on both an individual and a tribal level. In reading it, you will learn more of the horrors of forced relocation and will, we hope, be convinced that there is a better way to deal with this problem.

Acknowledgments

Many people have helped us in the preparation of this work. Greatest thanks go to those Navajos who took time to explain to us their feelings about compulsory relocation. We also wish to thank Peter MacDonald, Chairman of the Navajo Tribal Council, for writing the foreword, and Percy Deal, Executive Director of the Navajo-Hopi Land Dispute Commission, for assisting us in countless ways. Special thanks are due to Joseph Jorgensen for providing advice on methodological issues. For their assistance in preparing the manuscript for publication, we wish to thank Vera Beers and Joy Hansen for typing, Steve Brown for helping with the graphics, and Bill Jankowiak for preparing the index.

The opinions, conclusions, and recommendations in this book are those of the authors, and should not be viewed as reflecting the position of the Navajo Nation, the Institute for Development Anthropology, or any other organization.

CHAPTER 1

Introduction

The compulsory relocation of over 5,000 Navajos and up to ninety Hopis was mandated in 1974 by Public Law 93–531 and is currently being planned by the federal government's Navajo and Hopi Indian Relocation Commission. This relocation is part of a long-standing and ongoing conflict between the Navajo and Hopi people over land tenure and land usage in the former Joint Use Area (JUA) (see Figure 1). It is compulsory because the majority of the people do not wish to move. Thus, it is expensive in both financial and human terms. If the relocation is carried out according to congressional intent, the expected costs for housing and community facilities most likely will exceed $200 million, an estimate based on the Relocation Commission's own planning. Unfortunately, the expenditure of such a large sum of money cannot be expected to improve the lot of those Navajos who are involved in the project. On the contrary, relocation will increase Navajo dependence on welfare assistance because no money has been budgeted for economic development.

The current relocation policy of the United States government is summarized in the Uniform Relocation Assistance and Real Property Acquisition Policies Act of 1970. Restricted primarily to moving expenses, replacement housing, and advisory services for homeowners, tenants, businessmen, and farmers, this policy compares unfavorably with that in most other free world countries. Elsewhere, rural populations are usually given the option of moving as communities if they wish to do so. This is rarely the case in the United States, where relocatees are usually moved as families. Furthermore, though relocation authorities in many countries budget funds for economic development, social

1

Figure 1   The Navajo Reservation and Surrounding Towns. (Adapted
from Callaway et al. 1976:2.)

services, and housing, in the United States assistance is restricted
primarily to the procurement of decent, safe, and sanitary
replacement housing.

Although P.L. 93–531 improves upon the Uniform Relocation
Act of 1970 by emphasizing the need to provide Navajo relocatees with access to "related community facilities and services,

2

such as water, sewers, roads, schools and health facilities," no specific budgetary arrangements have been made to provide such services. And no mention is made of funds for an integrated program of economic development designed to improve conditions for the relocatees or even to maintain them at their former standard of living. As a result, we predict that the majority of adult Navajo women and the majority of Navajo men over forty years of age will be adversely affected by relocation.

While younger people can be expected to fare better than their elders because of improved access to education, even for them the adverse effects of relocation can be expected to be severe. This is due to the combination of the "freeze" on family and community improvement in the former Joint Use Area, the compulsory reduction of livestock, and the compulsory relocation. Navajos living within the Hopi portion of the former JUA have been under stress for over eighteen years. The *Healing* v. *Jones* decision in 1962 required the consent of both tribes for new construction. Although this decision did not specifically prohibit the building of new homes and community facilities, it limited such construction since joint consent was infrequently given, especially after 1966. On October 14, 1972 the District Court "issued an order of compliance which, among other things, stated, 'No new construction shall be permitted in the JUA without a permit issued jointly by the two tribes.' This effectively 'froze' development in the JUA" (Navajo and Hopi Indian Relocation Commission 1978: 42).

The freeze on new housing construction has contributed to the breakup of extended and nuclear families in a variety of ways. As they grow up and marry, young people have either had to move into crowded quarters with their parents or leave their homes entirely. In the former case, there are instances in which Navajos have blamed subsequent divorces on crowding and lack of privacy; in the latter case, the breakdown of the extended family and the increasing isolation of the elderly is accelerated. Compulsory destocking and the cancellation of grazing permits have added to the stress load, which has been further increased by the current relocation program. There is overwhelming

3

evidence that the combined stress has adversely affected the health of many Navajos. In this regard, a strong case can be made that the executive, legislative, and judicial branches of the United States government, in trying to resolve the Navajo-Hopi land dispute, have caused grave harm to the Navajo residents in the former JUA, especially those living on the Hopi side of the partition area. In the following chapters, we will present evidence that this harm, though unintentional, is a major infringement of the human rights of those involved, an infringement that demands rectification now that its magnitude has become known.

Much of the evidence presented here is new. In November 1978 the Navajo-Hopi Land Dispute Commission of the Navajo Nation requested that the Institute for Development Anthropology make a study of the human and economic costs of the Navajo relocation required by Public Law 93-531. The Institute was organized in June 1976 under the laws of the state of New York as a nonprofit group. Directed by Thayer Scudder, it carried out fieldwork within the Navajo Nation and adjacent urban centers in the states of Arizona and New Mexico in December 1978 and January 1979. Although this monograph is essentially an edited version of the report submitted by the Institute to the Navajo-Hopi Land Dispute Commission in March 1979, it has four additional features. The first is a foreword by Peter MacDonald, Chairman of the Navajo Tribal Council, which outlines the recent history of the land dispute from 1979 to July 1980. The second feature is an epilogue updating events to July 1981. The third feature (Appendix 4) is a multivariate analysis by David Aberle of the relationship of age, sex, education, place of relocation, and employment to the adjustment of the relocatees in our sample. The fourth feature is a methodological annex (Appendix 5) prepared by Aberle and Scudder, with the assistance of Joseph Jorgensen.

The purpose of the Institute's research was twofold. The first goal was to assess the whole range of expected effects associated with the compulsory relocation of 5,000 to 6,000 Navajo people from that portion of the former JUA partitioned to the Hopi tribe in 1977. For the purposes of analysis, the expected effects were divided into three categories: physiological, psychological, and sociocultural. However, these effects are in fact intricately interrelated in terms of their implications for individual Navajos and for Navajo households, as well as for extended kin groups, their associated chapters, and the Navajo Nation.

The second purpose of the research was to assess the advantages and disadvantages of the following three options: (1) compulsory relocation as currently mandated by P.L. 93–531; (2) amendment of P.L. 93–531; and (3) repeal of P.L. 93–531.

Based in part on interviews with adult members of 108 Navajo households, the majority of whom either have already been relocated or are under the threat of relocation, this monograph is the first major assessment of the actual and expected effects of the compulsory relocation of Navajo people. These effects are sufficiently serious that every effort should be made to launch a longitudinal monitoring study of the affected former JUA population should relocation proceed. The major purpose of such a study would be to identify stresses and problem areas as they arise so that they can be promptly dealt with. Although potential Hopi relocatees are fewer than one hundred, it is important that they be included within any such study. The Hopi relocatees are omitted from the present study simply because it was difficult to assess the effects upon them in a research project that was commissioned by the Navajo tribe.

The information presented within this monograph comes from two major sources. The first is the professional literature on the compulsory relocation of rural communities throughout the world, including Latin America, the United States and Canada, Africa, the Middle East, and Asia. This literature covers people of very different cultural backgrounds. In spite of this diversity, and in spite of the wide range of policies carried out by different relocation agencies, the response of relocatees to compulsory removal appears to be virtually the same the world over (Scudder 1973, 1976; Scudder and Colson 1981).

The second major source of information relates specifically to the Navajos. Although previous testimony to Congress and the

5

courts has assumed that the experience of other nations with compulsory relocation is applicable to the Navajos, a major purpose of this study was actually to assess the effects of removal on a number of Navajo households that have already undergone relocation, as well as to gauge the impact of P.L. 93–531 on Navajos threatened with relocation and on Navajo members of host communities, i.e., on residents of chapters* to which Navajo relocatees wish to move. One hundred and eight adult members of separate Navajo households were interviewed. These interviews were carried out in nine of the eleven Navajo chapters that are affected by the partition line as well as among relocatees in Flagstaff, Winslow, and St. Johns, Arizona, and Gallup and Fruitland, New Mexico. Of that number, thirty-four interviews were completed among urban relocatees, fourteen among rural relocatees, thirty-six among potential relocatees, and twenty-four among host community personnel.

Interviewing was not restricted to the former JUA Navajos who are affected by Public Law 93-531. It was also carried out among Navajos previously required to move from District 6, from the mining areas leased to the Peabody Coal Company on Black Mesa, and from the area south of Fruitland and Farmington set aside for the Navajo Indian Irrigation Project. Of the forty-eight relocated households in which one or more adult members were interviewed, thirty-eight (79 percent) had moved from the former JUA under the "voluntary" relocation program of the Navajo and Hopi Indian Relocation Commission.† This group constitutes slightly more than 50 percent of the households moved by the Commission through the end of 1978. No attempt was made to randomize or stratify the interview sample (Appendix 5). Instead, team members interviewed all relocatees

---

*Originally introduced by the Bureau of Indian Affairs in 1927, the Navajo chapter has become the basis for local government at the community level. Currently there are 102 chapters. Their officers are annually elected by popular vote.

†This program is for those Navajos who opt to move during the period when the Relocation Commission is planning a program of compulsory relocation or prior to the approval of that program by Congress.

who could be tracked down during the holiday season. As for potential relocatees and hosts, availability again was the major criterion for selection. Although this should be kept in mind when assessing the results of the study, we believe that the sample of interviewees accurately reflects the range of effects associated with compulsory relocation and the attitudes and concerns of potential relocatees and hosts. We believe this to be the case especially in regard to relocatees from the former JUA, not only because members of a majority of the involved households were interviewed but also because interviews were carried out in the three major urban centers to which these people had moved (Flagstaff, Winslow, and Gallup) as well as in on-reservation locales.

Since the majority of the interviews were carried out in Navajo, ideally the interview schedules should have been translated into Navajo. However, translation into Navajo involves methodological problems (see Appendix 5). Because we also had time constraints—the survey research had to be carried out during the Christmas holidays or not at all—interviewers translated questions into Navajo as they proceeded and then translated the answers back into English. We believe that the disadvantages of this approach were largely offset by the expertise and maturity of the team members and by the fact that Elizabeth Colson and Thayer Scudder spent several days in the field with two of the less experienced interviewers.

In addition to interviews, supplemental information relating to Navajo relocation was sought from scholars and officials associated with a variety of institutions, including the Bureau of Indian Affairs, the Indian Health Service, the Navajo Community College, the Navajo and Hopi Indian Relocation Commission, the Navajo Nation, and Northern Arizona University. (Their names and affiliations are listed in Appendix 1.)

To undertake the research described in this monograph, a carefully selected team of nine people (four Anglos and five Navajos) was recruited. The members of this team had expertise in studying the Navajo people, human stress, and the compulsory relocation of rural communities. Professor David Aberle of the

University of British Columbia, a well-known scholar of the Navajos, has conducted research on the Navajo Reservation since the 1940s. Kenneth Y. Begishe, a linguist teaching at the Navajo Community College, Shiprock, New Mexico, is one of the authors of *A Study of Navajo Perception of the Impact of Environmental Changes Relating to Energy Resource Development* (Schoepfle et al. 1978), which looked into Navajo reactions to relocation in connection with the Navajo Indian Irrigation Project as part of an Environmental Protection Agency study of Navajos who have been or may be affected by strip mining, shaft mining, and agribusiness. Professor Elizabeth Colson of the University of California, Berkeley, has extensive experience with World War II Japanese relocatees in the United States and dam relocatees in Africa. She is the author of *The Social Consequences of Resettlement* (1971). Clark Etsitty, a social worker at the Tuba City High School, has worked closely with Aberle in recent years. He carried out interviews in Piñon and Forest Lake Chapters and in Tuba City. Jennie Joe, who recently received a Ph.D. from the University of California in medical anthropology, is a registered nurse who also has an M.A. degree in public health. She and Betty Beetso Gilbert Tippeconnie completed the large majority of interviews among urban relocatees, while Tippeconnie also interviewed in Coal Mine Mesa Chapter. Mary E. D. Scudder, of Pacific Oaks College and Children's School, concentrated on the effects of relocation on children and the elderly. Professor Thayer Scudder, of the California Institute of Technology, has been studying forced community relocation in Africa, Asia, the Middle East, and the United States for over twenty-four years and is the author of a number of publications on compulsory community relocation throughout the world. Betty Beetso Gilbert Tippeconnie wrote her master's thesis at Arizona State University on the Navajos who had been relocated in 1972 from District 6. She worked for the Navajo and Hopi Indian Relocation Commission until her resignation in August 1978. Because of her knowledge, the research team was able to track down relocated households with comparative ease. Roy Walters was one of the interviewers associated with the Northern Arizona University report, *A*

Sociocultural Assessment of the Livestock Reduction Program in the Navajo-Hopi Joint Use Area (Wood, Vannette, and Andrews 1979), which was funded by the Bureau of Indian Affairs. His interviews were carried out in Red Lake Chapter.

The members of the study team were assisted over shorter periods of time by four employees of the Navajo Nation, who carried out additional interviews in Hard Rock, Teesto, Tolani Lake, and White Cone Chapters as well as in Gallup. These interviewers were Leon Begay, Freddie Howard,* and Dale Pete of the Navajo-Hopi Land Dispute Commission, and Bonnie Yellow Horse of the Navajo Nation's Paralegal Training Program. Where interviews were carried out in Navajo within the former JUA, in the large majority of cases interviewers were from the same chapter as the interviewees.

John Williamson, a graduate student in economics at the California Institute of Technology, joined the study team in January 1979. He coded the interviews, undertook the computer analysis, and provided other major assistance in preparing the report, including the collection of additional source material in Flagstaff and Window Rock. With Cynthia Carlson, also a graduate student in economics at Caltech, and Thayer Scudder, he independently ranked relocatees in regard to their adjustment to removal. In the writing of this monograph, David Aberle made a major contribution to several chapters, and Elizabeth Colson wrote much of chapter 7. Jeffrey B. Serena edited the original 1979 report during the spring of 1980, and Jerry Kammer graciously agreed to be the senior author of the epilogue in the summer of 1981.

---

*Deputy Executive Director of the Navajo-Hopi Land Dispute Commission at the time of the study, Freddie Howard resigned after his 1979 election to the Navajo Tribal Council.

CHAPTER 2

The Relocation of Low-Income Rural Communities with Strong Ties to the Land

Negative Effects of Relocation

The results of over twenty-five studies around the world indicate without exception that the compulsory relocation of low-income rural populations with strong ties to their land and homes is a traumatic experience. For the majority of those who have been moved, the profound shock of compulsory relocation is much like the bereavement caused by the death of a parent, spouse, or child. This multidimensional stress has been shown to have a number of negative effects.

Relocation undermines a people's faith in themselves—they learn, to their humiliation, that they are unable to protect their most fundamental interests. In the Navajo case, these interests include the preservation of their land (both for themselves and, of great importance, for their children), their homes, their system of livestock management with its associated lifestyle, and their links with the environment they were born to.

Partly because they have lost, at least temporarily, their self-respect and initiative, and because they did not request removal in the first place, many relocatees tend to become dependent on the agency or agencies responsible for their removal. This dependency syndrome has plagued innumerable resettlement programs, and it can be expected to plague Navajo relocation under P.L. 93–531, since funds currently are not budgeted, let alone allocated, for economic development and social services.

The trauma of relocation disrupts the family unit and the lives of each of its members. It undermines the influence and authority of the household head since he or she is shown to be incapable of preserving the family's lifestyle. Individual family members may suffer from severe depression. Violence, alcohol abuse, and mental and physical illness are all too often intimately associated with forced removal.

Relocation also undermines the influence and authority of local leaders. Throughout the world, politicians and officials find themselves in a "Catch-22" situation when their constituents are threatened with compulsory relocation. Since the majority of potential relocatees resist relocation in one way or another, their leaders are discredited if they cooperate with the relocation authorities. On the other hand, these leaders are also discredited if relocation occurs despite their resistance. In the Navajo case, both chapter and tribal officials are placed in an almost impossible position. If they withdraw land from the reservation for resettlement purposes, their actions will be seen as aiding and abetting relocation or as lowering the chances for passing amendments to P.L. 93–531, such as those that provide for purchase of additional land outside the reservation. On the other hand, if they resist relocation, their sincerity and effectiveness will still be questioned should relocation eventually occur. Under these circumstances, the present stance of the tribal authorities is understandable: it seems better to resist or attempt to modify relocation since in the long run such efforts may pay off, whereas agreeing to relocation now will discredit both the elected tribal council delegates from the former JUA and the tribal government itself.

Relocation creates serious conflicts between the relocatees, the hosts, and outsiders. These conflicts are characteristic of all rural projects involving compulsory relocation, and they can be expected to be especially serious among the Navajos. This is due to their restricted land base (with population densities more than double those in the areas surrounding the reservation, according to Gilbreath's 1973 analysis of the Navajo economy), their ranching style of life, and the current overgrazing of much of the reservation. When Navajo chapters hesitate and sometimes refuse to approve homesite leases for even small numbers of relocatees, they are not behaving in a uniquely unfeeling fashion. Indeed, such behavior is a common feature of all relocation projects in which relocatees wish to move or must move onto lands that are already occupied. Their arrival obviously reduces the per capita availability of land. It also increases the pressure on existing services—including water supplies, clinics, and schools—so that the hosts are often worse off after relocation.

The negative costs of relocation, like ripples, spread far beyond their points of origin. They demoralize families, break up kin groups, and divide whole communities and regions. In the Navajo case, these effects are already manifest and can be expected to influence the lives of the Navajo people for years to come.

Resistance to Relocation

The negative effects outlined above have been documented repeatedly in connection with programs of compulsory relocation. Possibly because they anticipate major disadvantages, the majority of relocatees the world over do not wish to move; indeed, they resist removal, sometimes violently. Unfortunately, it is impossible to forecast whether or not violence will occur in a specific case. In coping with the stress of relocation, potential relocatees often behave as if nothing were going to happen; rather, they continue to carry on their lives as in the past. We found some Navajos in the former JUA behaving in this fashion. For example, one household head told us, "Until the time comes, we will not discuss relocation." With no plans for relocation, he and the adult members of his family were part of that minority of household heads who had not yet applied for relocation benefits. An elderly man born before the turn of the century, he had no intention of moving. When such a family is forcibly evicted, it is impossible to predict what will happen, but the situation is potentially explosive.

In a similar situation in Africa studied by Colson and Scudder, a series of incidents under a "benevolent" relocation agency touched off violence that left eight potential relocatees dead and at least thirty-two injured. More recently, potential relocatees among the Kalingas in the Philippines have attacked government forces and scientists, killing at least twelve. Navajo threats of violence have already been heard. The octogenarian previously quoted threatened possible violence should relocation be forced. In addition, 16.1 percent (ten people) of the Navajos from the Hopi side of the partition line who sought mental health treatment from the Indian Health Service during a recent six-month period stated that the execution of relocation would be met with resistance (Martin Topper, personal communication). Such threats do not mean that physical violence against others will in fact occur, but the possibility cannot be discounted. Because compulsory relocation is a basic threat to the well-being of those involved, a "flashpoint" situation can occur with or without outside agitation.

Multidimensional Stress

Those who plan and execute programs of compulsory relocation are usually relatively educated, wealthy, and mobile individuals, often without strong ties to a particular geographical area or community. In the United States, they also tend to be the descendants of Anglo-Saxon or East European immigrants. They tend either to be unaware of, or at least to underestimate, the negative effects of compulsory relocation on less mobile, poorly educated, low-income populations, especially when such populations have a strong attachment to their homes, land, and livelihood, as is the case with the Navajo. The highly mobile planners are also apt to forget that their own movements tend to cause stress for their families, especially when children must leave school and associates and when nonworking spouses must leave friends and familiar surroundings for a new locale. Yet in such cases the move is freely discussed among family members and is usually of a voluntary nature.

13

While in the long run a majority of those who are subject to compulsory relocation may become better off (though not necessarily because of relocation), in the short run the effects of relocation are invariably adverse. Furthermore, the relocatees' position in life can be expected to improve only if they have access to training programs and employment opportunities. These developmental components are not provided for under P.L. 93–531, despite the fact that the former Joint Use Area has one of the highest unemployment rates in the United States (76 percent of those sixteen and older have no wage or salary employment, according to Wood, Vannette, and Andrews 1979: 104).

Compulsory relocation invariably involves multidimensional stress. This stress begins as soon as the first rumors of possible relocation arise. It increases during the months immediately preceding removal and remains at a high level during much of the transition period. Throughout this time, relocatees often behave like those who are mourning the death of a loved one. They turn in upon themselves, relying on family members and close friends. They cling to the familiar and try to recreate their old routines and lifestyles in their new home. Relocatees behave as if their world is a closed system; they try to move the shortest distance possible and then only into familiar surroundings. This phenomenon has been commonly observed in urban redevelopment projects throughout the United States: whenever possible, relocatees move into adjacent neighborhoods.

Clinging to the familiar in the form of known persons, routines, and surroundings would appear to be a means of coping with the multidimensional stress of relocation. In a world turned upside down, the familiar provides assurance until the transition period comes to an end. After that, the individual—if he or she is still alive—is able to turn outward again. For the purposes of our analysis, multidimensional stress can be broken down into three components: physiological stress, psychological stress, and sociocultural (including economic) stress. These three components are synergistically interrelated.

Physiological stress results in increased morbidity rates, for both mental and physical illness. It may also result in increased mortality rates.

Psychological stress has two aspects, one directed toward the past and the other directed toward the future. The first has been labeled by Fried (1963) as the "grieving for a lost home" syndrome. It is especially serious among the elderly and among younger women, although its effect on children has never been adequately researched. The second aspect is a strong anxiety about the future, including a feeling of uncertainty that can be most debilitating. In situations of uncertainty, people feel that they are out of context. Because they do not know "the rules of the game," they cannot calculate the odds associated with different coping strategies—so risk-taking becomes impossible. They cease to explore, become disoriented, and draw in upon themselves. With the loss of their independence, initiative, and self-respect, such relocatees tend to develop a dependency relationship with the agency or agencies that moved them, a relationship that is hard to break and that delays the end of the transition period.

Sociocultural stress is not as well understood as the other two components. It is caused by the disruption, disorganization, and simplification of the behavioral patterns, institutions, and organizational processes of a community and of the society of which it is a part. A major aspect of this sort of stress is the undermining of local leadership. Another aspect is the temporary or permanent disruption of established behavioral patterns, including forms of livelihood that give meaning to life. These are stopped with relocation because they are tied to particular pieces of land. For instance, there are special sites where wild plants are gathered for eating and ritual purposes; other sites are reserved for carrying out certain rituals. In the Navajo case, the cessation of sheep herding is especially serious, particularly for the elderly; it signals the disappearance of the whole way of life associated with the ownership of grazing permits and the care of livestock.

The types of multidimensional stress outlined above are associated with the transition period that invariably accompanies compulsory relocation. For the majority of relocatees, this period extends at least two years from the date of relocation. It seldom lasts more than a single generation, since children born in the relocation setting tend to adapt to that setting. The Navajos, however, may follow a path similar to that of the Palestinian Arabs. In both cases, there is a very strong identification with their land and an overriding desire by adults to pass that land on to their children. For these people, inability to accept expulsion from their homes may go on for several generations.

CHAPTER 3

A History of the Land Dispute
and Its Effects on Local Navajos

Introduction

In terms of expected negative effects, the most grievous relocation of Navajos in the present century is the former Joint Use Area relocation required by Public Law 93–531. This is not solely due to the large number of people involved but also to the special circumstances surrounding the former JUA.

The best current sources of information on Navajos living in the former JUA were published in 1978 (before that date, little information on this isolated and conflict-ridden region was available). These sources are the needs assessment reports prepared by the Bureau of Indian Affairs (1978) and the Navajo Nation (1978a) and *A Sociocultural Assessment of the Livestock Reduction Program in the Navajo-Hopi Joint Use Area*, a report that was written by Wood, Vannette, and Andrews (1979) in fulfillment of a BIA contract. The Wood, Vannette, and Andrews report is comprehensive and especially relevant; we have drawn heavily on it in this chapter. It is based on both published and unpublished secondary source materials and on a household survey carried out in late 1977. In the survey, 146 household heads were interviewed, approximately 7 percent of the former JUA household heads listed in BIA records. Drawn on a random basis, these individuals were broadly distributed in twelve of the fourteen chapters that utilize land within the former JUA, including all eleven chapters that have some land on the Hopi side of the partition line.

The former JUA lies within the western portion of the Navajo Reservation, an area that historically lags behind the eastern portion in educational facilities and economic opportunities. Even today, when the Navajo tribe is following a "growth center development strategy," the major growth centers, aside from Tuba City, are in the east. As for the former JUA, its development lags still further behind. According to the BIA, only 68.6 miles of roads are paved in this 2,846 square-mile area. The remaining 637.7 miles of roads are unimproved dirt tracks that are "virtually impassable during the months of December, January, February, March, April, July, August, and September, or eight months of the year. By virtue of this fact, this area is the most neglected, the most isolated and the most desperately in need of attention of any section of the reservation" (Bureau of Indian Affairs 1978: 32). As we shall see, efforts by the United States government to resolve the long-standing Navajo-Hopi land dispute have, unintentionally, increased the poverty of the area, especially through the freeze on new construction.

Figure 2 shows the age-sex structure of the Navajo population in the former JUA. The population is relatively young, with 47 percent and 37 percent under the age of fifteen in 1970 and 1977, respectively; the proportions of persons sixty-five and over in those two years were 4 percent and 7 percent. The dependency ratio—i.e., the proportion of dependent children and elders to more active producers—is high, as it is for the Navajo Reservation as a whole. However, further analysis of the 1977 data by Wood, Vannette, and Andrews indicates that the former JUA has the highest dependency ratio within the reservation. While this is primarily a factor of the large number of children, it is also due to "an ever increasing proportion of aged persons" (1979: 41). These conclusions have several major implications for relocation. First, the large number of dependents puts additonal pressure for support on an already highly stressed adult population. Second, the increasing proportion of elderly persons is a matter for concern since compulsory relocation is particularly stressful for this group. Finally, the large number of children is also a cause for concern, especially since very little is known about the effects of

*Figure 2   Age-Sex Structure of the Former Joint Use Area Popula-
tion. (From Wood, Vannette, and Andrews 1979: 39.)*

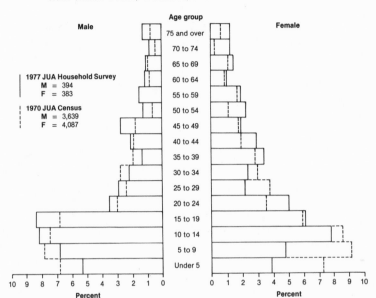

relocation on children. In comparison to the elderly, they may be
"the forgotten victims."

Although young people must go out of the area for schooling
and to find work, the population is residentially stable, with a
close identification with the former JUA that extends over the
generations. In view of the popular misconception of the Navajos
as "nomads moving across the landscape" without strong ties to
the land, this is a very important finding. In the Wood, Vannette,
and Andrews survey (1979), 88.6 percent of the household
members had lived at their present locales for 75 to 100 percent
of their lives. Most changes in residence that had occurred were
within the boundaries of the former JUA, and most residents
tended to marry within this area.

Like Navajos elsewhere, former JUA residents derive their

19

meager income from a variety of activities including livestock management and farming, weaving and silversmithing, wage employment, and general assistance (welfare). Livestock management and farming were the most common activities of the households in the Wood, Vannette, and Andrews survey: 91 percent had stock prior to the compulsory destocking that began in 1976, while 45 percent farmed. Although livestock produced approximately 25 percent of the households' total aggregate income (through home consumption, wool production, and meat sales), the major source of income was wages, followed by general assistance. However, of those family members aged sixteen years or older, only 23.7 percent (33.5 percent of the men and 14.8 percent of the women) had been able to find wage employment. This proportion is lower than that of the rest of the reservation; it must surely be one of the lowest wage employment rates in the United States. It is not surprising, then, that 71.3 percent of the households surveyed received some form of general assistance in the ten to eleven months prior to being interviewed.

Educational services, like employment opportunities, were also inadequate. According to the BIA, 78.5 percent of the parents of former JUA students have had no schooling at all. Though the current demand for education is high within the area, only one local school goes as far as the eighth grade.

Historical Background

The former Joint Use Area was created in 1882 by an executive order of President Chester A. Arthur. It consists of approximately 1.8 million acres (2,846 square miles) surrounding the Hopi Reservation (District 6), which was enlarged to its present size in 1943. Though set aside for both the Hopis and "such other Indians as the Secretary of the Interior may see fit to settle thereon," an unknown number of Navajos lived in the area at that time, and over the years their number has increased. According to the 1976 BIA census, 11,689 Navajos (roughly 8 percent of the entire Navajo population) lived in the former JUA, as opposed to fewer than 500 Hopis. Under these circumstances, Hopi access to the former JUA has been severely restricted, with the result that the Hopi Tribal Council has been seeking a congressional solution to the problem for many years. In 1958 Congress enacted Public Law 85–547, which set in motion actions to adjudicate Navajo and Hopi claims to the former JUA.

A district court of three judges was established, and it released its opinion (*Healing* v. *Jones*) in the fall of 1962. According to the court's judgment, it had no jurisdiction to partition the former JUA; rather, both tribes should share the surface and subsurface rights subject to the trust title of the United States. Following this decision, the Hopi Tribal Council sought to protect its surface rights from further Navajo encroachment. These new Hopi initiatives ultimately resulted in a series of federal actions with profound repercussions for the social and economic fabric of the former JUA.

On July 1, 1966, the Commissioner of Indian Affairs instituted a freeze on all significant developments in the former Joint Use Area unless they were approved by the Hopis. These included mineral explorations, mining, rights of way, and any activity involving trading, permits, leases, or licenses (home construction, construction of community facilities, schools, and so on). Although Navajos were allowed to upgrade existing housing, and a few new houses were built (with BIA assistance prior to 1972), this freeze on construction in the former JUA has been bitterly resented by the Navajos. For example, in outlining their needs for a better future, members of the Red Lake Chapter listed "decent housing with sewer and electrical facilities" as their first priority (Navajo Nation 1978a).

The court-ordered freeze has set back the development of one of the poorest areas in the United States. In the opinion of the BIA and many Navajos, it has also played havoc with Navajo social organization by raising the divorce rate and undermining the extended family system. Because of the freeze, many families were not able to build new housing for their children as they matured, married, and began new families on their own. This

21

lack of housing, along with the lack of job and other economic opportunities within the former JUA (in itself partially attributable to the freeze), has caused an acceleration in the movement of new families away from this area. These families tended to settle off the reservation in such "border" towns as Flagstaff, thus physically separating the generations and, in the opinion of those who remained behind, weakening the extended family. Ironically, those who moved found themselves in a precarious situation, since it was not clear until December 1978, when the Relocation Commission broadened its eligibility criteria, that such families would qualify for relocation benefits under P.L. 93–531.

While some new families moved out of the former JUA to seek homes and jobs, others moved into the existing housing of parents, in-laws, and other relatives. This caused overcrowding that stressed family relationships, which some Navajos blame for the subsequent breakdown of their marriages. For example, one woman in our sample of relocatees blamed her 1972 divorce on the problem of not having a home of her own. She and her husband had moved in with her father's family in overcrowded conditions that led to conflict. Both this woman and her mother stated that other families within their own extended kin group also broke up for the same reason. In the mother's words, the situation was "very disgraceful and shameful, and very embarrassing to talk about." The implication was that such overcrowding led to disputes and to behavior that was detrimental to the entire kin group.

The freeze did not complete the process of federally mandated economic paralysis in the former JUA. Instead, more court action followed. On October 14, 1972, the United States District Court issued an order of compliance that not only reaffirmed the limitations on construction but required the reduction of the 120,000 sheep units* in the former JUA to half of carrying capacity, or half of 16,000 sheep units, in one year. This order

---

*One sheep unit consists of a sheep or a goat whereas a cow is equivalent to four sheep units and a horse (or burro) to five.

was reaffirmed by the passage of P.L. 93–531 on December 22, 1974, and by a court action on October 14, 1975. Destocking finally began in 1976. Based on range management studies, the BIA decided that the condition of the range was so bad that approximately 90 percent of the existing stock would have to be removed. The BIA encouraged sales by purchasing stock at 150 percent of its appraised value. In the southeastern portion of the former JUA, where the destocking and range rehabilitation program was initiated, visible results have been achieved. With approximately 90 percent of the stock removed, the range has begun to recover. During 1977, grazing permits were reintroduced, though only on an annual basis. In 1978, restoration had proceeded to the point that permit holders were allowed to double the livestock listed on their 1977 permits—bringing them up, on the average, to about 20 percent of the livestock units they had prior to destocking.

Although Navajo household heads in the Wood, Vannette, and Andrews survey said they did not believe that the range had deteriorated over the years, the evidence for environmental degradation is overwhelming. Improved range management, including an integrated approach to water and food supply and a degree of intensification through approaches to supplemental feeding, is essential. However, there is also no doubt that both destocking and the previous threat of destocking have been a most stressful experience for the Navajos. To them livestock management is a way of life that has little to do with the actual commercial value of their animals, although even this has been underestimated by outsiders (Wood, Vannette, and Andrews 1979; Russell 1978). The economic and sociocultural values associated with livestock are documented in Navajo autobiographies, in scholarly publications, and by the tremendous importance that Navajos place on grazing permits. This last has been carefully studied by Begishe in the Burnham area. Grazing permits were first introduced by the BIA in 1940 after the compulsory destocking of the 1930s. These permits can be sold, although in fact the large majority are either retained by the original owners or inherited by their kin. In view of Navajo attitudes toward livestock, even the

23

mere threat of destocking is stressful; the actual impact of the cancellation of grazing permits is difficult for an outsider to comprehend.

Household heads interviewed during the Wood, Vannette, and Andrews study emphasized four effects of compulsory livestock reduction:

> Economic hardship was mentioned most often (37.7 percent). As one respondent noted, "We depend on sheep for our meat and food, [our] source of income; it's as a bank; we use it for when we want money, pride, and survival." Another person said, "All livestock owners will be under the lower standard of living income. They will have no credits, no wool, no livestock to sell, no jobs and starve, of course." The concern over having no money, no job, and no income led a number of persons to voice a fear of not being able to support their families, and of living in poverty. One respondent said, "We are poverty-stricken. We are going back to [the] way it was before the Long Walk."
>
> A second perceived impact was that of starvation and an inadequate diet. Approximately 20 percent (19.8) of the responses identified this concern. Comments such as "[we will] starve and have no money," "people will go hungry," and "children will starve" were repeatedly voiced. Some respondents also reported feeling their "health had gone down due to [a] shortage of proper food like meat and stew."
>
> Loss of a "way of life," culture, and traditional values was a third concern expressed in 18.2 percent of the responses. Related to this, people were concerned fighting and conflict would arise; and there was sadness voiced over not being able to provide sheep to squaw dances, and not being able to help clan members. Mutton hunger was also reported by some persons, as was a concern for rearing their children. As one individual expressed it, "We are experiencing homesickness, loss of our livestock, and most importantly, our way of teaching responsibilities to our children."
>
> The fourth concern reported was that of loneliness and depression. Approximately 15 percent of the responses identified this effect. Death, loss of strength, and drinking behavior were also associated with these conditions. One person eloquently summarized his feelings as follows: "Sheep is life. Who can live if their life is taken away?" [1979: 198–99]

The profound stresses of destocking and the construction freeze imposed on Navajo residents of the former JUA have been exacerbated by the confusion attendant upon the actual partition process. The Judgment of Partition on February 10, 1977 (Figure 3) established a partition line and permitted no new construction in the former JUA except by permission of the tribe to which a particular piece of land had been mandated. However, the partition line was temporarily voided on May 15, 1978 by the Ninth United States Circuit Court of Appeals because of questions that had arisen about the survey of certain former JUA boundary lines. Although an interim line was drawn the following August, the final line has yet to be established.* Meanwhile, the Navajo tribe launched a major effort to amend Public Law 93-531.

Needless to say, this complicated history of events has been most confusing to the Navajo residents of the former JUA. Given conflicting information by representatives of different agencies and even by different staff members within the same agency, the large majority continue to hope that somehow it will be possible for them to remain in their customary use areas. Rumors are rife. When the partition line was temporarily voided, some potential relocatees thought this meant that relocation would not be required, an impression that was strengthened by a temporary cessation of the Relocation Commission's program of "voluntary" relocations. The Commission itself has contributed to the uncertainty of the potential relocatees because of rapid turnover in staff (since individual staff members present information in different ways) and because of indecision over exactly who will be eligible for relocation benefits. The resulting confusion, compounded by the tangle of federal statutes and litigation, has created an atmosphere of uncertainty and fear.

---

*An order of final adjudication was issued by the United States District Court for Arizona on April 18, 1979. The Navajo and Hopi Indian Relocation Commission has two years from that date to submit its relocation report and plan to Congress. If the report is approved, compulsory relocation under the plan will take place over the next five years.

Figure 3   Former Joint Use Area and District 6 (Hopi Indian Reservation). (Adapted from Navajo and Hopi Indian Relocation Commission 1978: 2, Fig. 1, and 23, Fig. 5.)

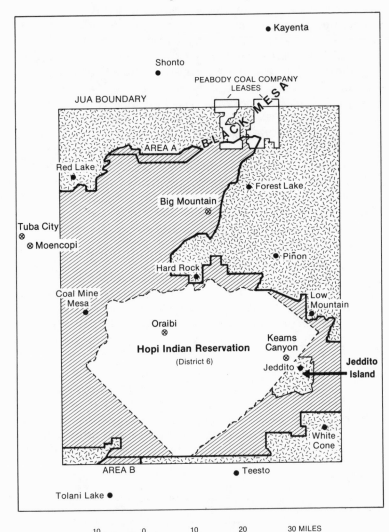

10   0   10   20   30 MILES

Navajo (Side of Partition Line)
Hopi (Side of Partition Line)
● Navajo Chapter House
⊗ Other Locations Mentioned in Text

The Stressful Effects of the Land Dispute on Local Navajos

It is hard to overemphasize the extremely stressful effects of this long and bitter conflict on the Navajo residents of the area. Not only is the stress load high, but it has been building since 1958 and especially since 1972. It is also accompanied by an increasing resentment against the United States government. According to Wood, Vannette, and Andrews, government intervention is perceived by the Navajos as the number-one factor shifting them toward the "worst kind of life" (1979: 223–25). Livestock reduction, relocation, fencing, harassment, and the land-dispute issue are all reported as examples of this intervention.

Referring more specifically to the stress component of life within the former JUA, the 1978 BIA needs assessment report states: "The people living in the Joint Use Area have been under psychological and social stress unparalleled elsewhere on the Reservation." This has resulted in "a breakdown of family ties, the disintegration of the nuclear family, [and] a sharp rise in alcoholism, suicide, and misdemeanor offenses. The social needs are monumental. Many problems have developed in this period which have never existed in the past" (1978: 168).

Most of these BIA statements are general impressions, since there is not enough statistical information to verify them. However, recent data collected by Martin Topper of the Indian Health Service division of the United States Public Health Service indicates that a serious mental health problem does exist among Navajos living on the Hopi side of the partition line. Topper's methodology was to obtain information on all former JUA residents who sought assistance for mental health problems from the various Indian Health Service facilities that surround the former JUA or, in the case of Keams Canyon, from the facilities that are within District 6. Information was collected in 1978 over approximately twenty-five weeks between July 1 and December 18; the number of walk-in patients from whom information was gathered totaled eighty. Diagnosis was made separately by professional and paraprofessional staff. Topper concludes the following:

> Navajo residents of the former JUA who face the prospect of relocation have a higher incidence of mental health complaints than either residents of the former JUA who will not be relocated or than Navajos in general. In addition, it is clear that Navajo patients from both sides of the former JUA are presenting complaints which indicate as patient populations they are suffering from depression at a rate that is over twice the rate for the reservation as a whole. Furthermore, almost all of the patients who have been assigned a diagnostic impression of depression also have presented voluntary complaints about the land dispute or its components: the building freeze, stock reduction, or relocation. Finally, it has been shown that a great deal of the patient population is composed of people over forty, most of whom are potential relocatees. [1979: 16–17]

In comparison to former JUA Navajos who do not have to relocate because they live on the Navajo side of the partition line, the population of potential relocatees has "eight times the mental health service utilization rate as non-relocatees" within the former JUA. Topper's survey was carried out after the partition line had been demarcated by the District Court. Presumably one reason the utilization rate was so low among nonrelocatees was because the threat of removal had finally been lifted from them; at the same time, a program was implemented on the Navajo side of the partition line to improve housing and community services. The prolonged period of stress for these people was over.

During the period of Topper's study, patients living on the Hopi side of the partition line accounted for 4.59 percent of the case load from the entire reservation, even though they constituted only 2.4 percent of the population. Although 39 percent of the sample had no education, 26 percent had eleven to fourteen years of schooling. In other words, both educated and uneducated Navajos were affected. The majority of patients (of whom 55 percent were female) were over forty years of age.

Sixty-one percent of the patients from the Hopi side of the partition line complained of severe distress on account of the land dispute. Those seeking assistance included five ceremonial practitioners (medicine men), four of whom came from the Hopi side. Though one of the five suffered from a condition not directly related to the land dispute, the others "had severe stress due to the dispute. Three said they were overloaded with work or could no longer practice due to the dispute" (Martin Topper, personal communication). This suggests that the "native system of health care is beginning to have difficulty dealing with" the land dispute (Topper 1979: 9).

Other information on reactions to stress is more vague, but it points in the same direction as Topper's information. Some BIA personnel believe that the land dispute has contributed to a rapid rise in alcohol abuse among residents of the former JUA. High school students from the former JUA appear to be disproportionately represented among those involved in major drinking incidents at the Many Farms High School (Bureau of Indian Affairs 1978: 168).

The death rate among the ninety Navajos evicted from District 6 in 1972 has been exceptionally high. Between December 1972 and the end of 1978, four of the five relocatees who were over the age of fifty-five at the time of the eviction died, along with five other adults between the ages of twenty and fifty-five. Together these nine people represent nearly 25 percent of the adult population. Six of the nine deceased were women, three of whom were struck and killed by vehicles in reservation border towns. At the time of death, two of these women were under thirty; the other was forty-one. According to Topper (personal communication), such deaths may reflect a self-destructive urge that is associated with the type of depression correlated with compulsory relocation.

In sum, all sources of information available to us, including our own interviews, which are analyzed in the chapters that follow, indicate that the impact of the long-standing land dispute has been exceedingly stressful for the local Navajo residents. Not only has the stress load been high, but much of it can be directly attributed to attempts by the United States government to resolve the dispute, especially over the past twenty years. In addition to the present relocation program and the long-standing uncertainty over land tenure, stress can be attributed to three other factors: the freeze on new housing and other construction within the former JUA; the long-standing threat of compulsory livestock reduction, which was finally made real when de-stocking began in 1976; and the uncertainty as to whether or not the relocatees will be able to move elsewhere on the reservation.

CHAPTER 4

Relocation and Land
Among the Navajos

Numbers of Relocatees and Potential Relocatees

A surprisingly large number of Navajo people currently live under the threat of compulsory relocation or have been relocated within the past ten years. Perhaps half of those involved live in that portion of the former Joint Use Area partitioned to the Hopis. The original estimate of their number was approximately 3,500. In its December 1978 Interim Progress Report, the Navajo and Hopi Indian Relocation Commission raised this estimate to 4,800. For a number of reasons, this too can be considered an underestimate of the total to be relocated. First, in all cases of compulsory relocation of which we are aware, the final number of people actually relocated exceeds previous estimates. This is due in part to the difficulty of getting accurate census material from suspicious populations of poorly educated people.

Second, the figure of 4,800 does not take into account the increase in population that will take place during the next five to seven years. Assuming that 350 people have already moved, a conservative estimate (at 2 percent per annum) of population increase for the remaining 4,450 people during the next twelve months would yield an additional eighty-nine people. Although the figures would be lower for succeeding years because of a gradual reduction in the number of people through ongoing relocation, it is obvious that over 5,000 people will be involved before the relocation exercise is complete.

Third, the Relocation Commission's figure of 4,800 is based on the assumption that 1,200 household heads (with each household averaging four members) would qualify for relocation benefits from the 1,922 heads of household who had filed applications by December 1978. This is an acceptance rate of 60 to 65 percent. More recently, however, the Relocation Commission staff estimates that up to 90 percent of the 120 to 130 applicants currently being processed will qualify, while their overall estimate of acceptance (which we suspect is still too low) has risen to 65 to 75 percent. Meanwhile, the number of applicants can be expected to rise above 2,000 once known holdouts submit applications. A 75 percent acceptance rate from 2,000 household heads would raise the number of relocatees to 6,000 people. We consider this number to be a more realistic estimate for planning purposes.*

The possibility of compulsory relocation also threatens several thousand Navajos who live within the Moencopi area claimed by the Hopi.† Elsewhere, up to ninety Navajo families will be required to move in connection with the Navajo Indian Irrigation Project. Some of these families will be moving for the second time—they were displaced on a previous occasion by the operations of the Navajo Mine near Fruitland. Other mining operations on Black Mesa and near Window Rock have disrupted a smaller number of Navajo households and will require movement of others in the future. Bearing this in mind, if we then

---

*After this report was submitted to the Navajo-Hopi Land Dispute Commission, the Navajo and Hopi Indian Relocation Commission raised the estimate from 4,800 to 5,600. By May 1980 the Relocation Commission had received 2,423 applications from household heads (Navajo and Hopi Indian Relocation Commission 1980). We would not be surprised if the figure of 6,000 Navajo relocatees also proves to be an underestimate.

†This is the dispute referred to in Chairman MacDonald's foreword. Its basis is a 1934 Act of Congress dealing with the Arizona boundaries of the Navajo Reservation which reserves the land for both Navajo and other resident Indians. Because of this clause in the Act, the Hopi tribal council has claimed half of the disputed land. The Navajos, on the other hand, assert that the Hopi have a reasonable claim only to a much smaller amount of land around the Hopi village of Moencopi near Tuba City.

consider future plans for coal gasification and uranium mining, especially in the eastern portion of the Navajo Reservation and adjacent areas of New Mexico, the number of Navajos under the threat of eviction for one reason or another may reach 10 percent of the total population of the Navajo Reservation. This is a terrible burden to put on a people with a unique relationship to their land.

The Navajo Relationship to the Land

INTRODUCTION

For most Navajos the idea of relocation is deeply disturbing, even when it involves voluntary relocation to urban centers, such as that which occurred under the Bureau of Indian Affairs' urban relocation program. In that case, however, those involved could always return to the reservation and to their own homes and chapters either permanently or for visits. Partition is totally different; it removes the land forever by giving it to the Hopis. For most Navajos this is entirely unacceptable, and for many it is incomprehensible. Loss of land through relocation deprives the Navajos of their birthright, their livelihood, their proper social relationships, and their familiar and beloved surroundings. It also deprives them of significant places where they can make religious offerings to maintain the correct relationship with the supernatural. Indeed, it upsets the order of nature itself.

LAND AS A BIRTHRIGHT

Navajos belong to the land of their people by virtue of birth; they believe they have been put on this earth to use the land that has been provided for their use by supernatural beings. But individual Navajos can exercise their *general* birthright only through *specific* customary rights to use an area. These are acquired by living where one's parents are living or where they

33

lived until death, or by moving to live with a spouse who occupies land where his or her parents lived or are living. Except for moves to town or to administrative enclaves, most movement is made as a result of marriage or the exercise of kinship claims. Thus, if a Navajo gives up any claim to the former JUA, he loses his general birthright to the Navajo country since he no longer has any specific claim. Well aware of this danger, some of those we interviewed were especially concerned that relocation would effectually exile their children from the reservation.

LAND AND LIVELIHOOD

Until the recent drastic reduction, most Navajos in the former JUA had some livestock. From these they gained up to 25 percent of their livelihood; they also practiced some subsistence farming. As presently conceived, relocation plans allow almost no relocated Navajos the possibility of keeping livestock or of farming, in contrast to the Relocation Commission's plans for Hopi relocatees. The value of livestock to Navajos has been consistently underrated by non-Navajo administrators and by most observers. Livestock provides food, cash income, provender for important ceremonies, and gifts for exchange with kin. Its value for home consumption is the cost of an equivalent amount of meat of equal nutritional value at retail market prices—its replacement cost, not its sale value on the hoof. Since Navajos eat virtually the entire carcass—including the liver, tongue, brains, kidneys, and intestines—the nutritional value is higher than an equivalent weight of muscle meat. In addition, the wool is woven, and its value is greatly increased by the work of the craftswoman who sells the finished goods. It is common to underrate this economic benefit on the grounds that a weaver's payment per hour is low, but since most women who weave have no other income-producing possibilities except caring for the livestock, income from weaving is obviously significant. A good weaver can earn several thousand dollars a year, and large rugs are often sold for $500 or more.

Because it provides income and because it is the economic

activity they know best, Navajos say that caring for livestock gives their lives purpose. Old people with no stock to care for feel useless; old people who have stock feel vital. People with stock care for them in all weather, even into their eighties and nineties. "Sheep is all we know," they say. "Everything we learned was from caring for the sheep." Relocation deprives them of income, adequate food, and purpose in life. They are fully conscious of the connection between the loss of land and the loss of stock.

LAND AND SOCIAL LIFE

Navajo social life in the former JUA is built on a unit considerably larger than the family. A set of closely related nuclear families (usually a woman, her husband, and her daughters and their husbands) forms a cluster of dwellings. A set of matrilineally connected clusters occupies a contiguous stretch of territory, which may include some twenty-five square miles or more, or two or more such stretches of land for summer and winter range. The largest amount of mutual aid occurs between the families of a cluster, but more important assistance also occurs among the clusters of the larger set, usually called an outfit or residence group by Anglos (no one Navajo term can be given). Piecemeal relocation of families destroys this entire fabric.

The distribution of kinship groups on the land is a map of social relationships, and one might say that kinship relationships and relationships to the land are a single phenomenon. Since these relationships are threatened by relocation, those Navajos who can face the idea of relocation (not the idea of actually being relocated, but the general concept of relocation) say that if it is to be done, whole residence groups or even whole communities should be moved so that old relationships may be retained on new land. This cannot be done by moving the people to subdivisions near chapter houses as currently planned by the Navajo and Hopi Indian Relocation Commission's Interim Progress Report (1978: 59–137). Since individual households would have access to less than an acre apiece, they could not herd livestock.

35

NAVAJO LOVE OF THE LAND

The Navajo love of the land is very strong. In the 1920s, a linguist collected some older Indians' memories of Fort Sumner, where the majority of the Navajos were interned between 1864 and 1868. They recalled the Navajos' poetic laments as they mourned the loss of their beloved country. Among the places they mourned was Black Mountain, the heart of the former Joint Use Area.

Navajos love the minute details of their homeland. They have many lookout places from which to enjoy its beauty. In the recent court cases and congressional hearings, the idea has been promulgated that the Navajos are homeless wanderers unattached to the land. However, the large regions occupied by close relatives of a single clan do not correspond with nomadism. Seasonal moves within a use area do not constitute nomadism, even if a different dwelling is occupied for each season. Swiss and Scandinavian farmers move from winter to summer pastures on the same holding, and so do the Navajos. For older people, whether living in their own birthplace or that of their spouse, a lifetime of close relationship with a particular tract of land creates bonds that they dread to see severed, or cannot believe will be severed.

Navajo veterans from the former JUA are especially concerned about losing the land they love. According to the Navajo Office of Veterans Affairs, there are approximately 12 to 13,000 living Navajo veterans. The Navajos are proud of this record of military service to the United States. They are also proud that the Navajo language was used as a secret code (one that was never cracked) during World War II.

Although we do not have information on the proportion of veterans in the former JUA, we would suspect it to be similar to that for the reservation as a whole. The walls of Navajo houses in the former JUA often display American flags and pictures of servicemen. But in fighting for the United States, Navajos have seen their service as part of a moral relationship of reciprocity: they have fought for the land of the American people, and they expect the American people to help them struggle for their own land. Accordingly, veterans are deeply distressed to learn that in spite of their war effort the United States is now planning to evict them.

In interviews, Navajos from the former JUA have specifically mentioned that they feel their past military service has not been appreciated by the government. One veteran, wounded in France and now a medicine man on the Hopi side of the partition line, put it this way: "I feel that we have done valuable things for the country and now they want us to move from this simple piece of land" (Kammer 1980: 198). Another veteran, noting that his ancestors had eluded Kit Carson's troops to remain in the former JUA throughout the captivity at Fort Sumner, asked the Relocation Commissioners at one meeting what they thought about "relocating people who didn't go on the Long Walk" (Kammer 1980: 177).

Some of our interviewees made similar statements. According to one, "our language was used to win the war. [Our relatives] carried rifles to protect the white man, but yet they do not consider this service and we are being told to relocate." Another stated that a number of his relatives had served in World War II, including one brother who died from his wounds. All, in his opinion, had joined up "to protect their lands and families. As a result, the war was won and our language was used also. Now the whole land dispute issue seems to be unaffected [by the fact that] our relatives have participated [in the war]."

THE RELIGIOUS SIGNIFICANCE OF THE LAND

Many Navajos consider the religious significance of the land on the Hopi side of the partition line to be an important issue, even the preeminent issue, of the land dispute. The Navajos do not, however, like to discuss the supernatural, so this aspect of the relocation is rarely voiced in public hearings and other forums. Nevertheless, the Relocation Commission contracted with John J. Wood and Walter M. Vannette of Northern Arizona University to investigate the significance of Navajo sacred places near Big Mountain on the Hopi side of the partition line. In their report, they noted:

> Federal recognition, legislative treatment, enforcement proce-
> dures, and administrative policy directives also have been
> limited with respect to sacred places. This limitation may be a
> result of failing to perceive what constitutes Navajo reality of
> sacredness of place. Although variation does exist, it would
> seem that there is a symbiotic relation between belief, place,
> participation through use, and occupancy. To segment this
> interdependent relationship by allowing for *access* to a sacred
> location is to subtract occupancy, and, perhaps, a degree of
> participation through use. A clear example of this segmenting
> process exists in the case of Healing vs. Jones. Here visitation to
> special religious places was recognized, but the court found
> that this in no way constituted occupancy nor did it establish
> exclusive interest in these places. This position seems to sever
> the links between the parts which constitute the symbolic
> sacredness of place and, therefore, the right to preserve the
> integrity of such places. However well intended, it appears
> that this position is an implicit infringement upon the exercise
> of free religious belief and meaningful spiritual observance.
> Big Mountain residents have been resistant in part because
> they perceive these conditions and positions as being restric-
> tive and precluding their basic human rights as set forth by
> law. [1979: 2–3]

This "symbiotic relation between belief, place, participation through use, and occupancy" can be generalized throughout the reservation. As some Navajos tell their origin myths, the Navajo people emerged from three lower worlds to appear finally on this one. They traveled on the authority of supernatural beings who told them why they should move and where. These beings gave them the use of the land, made it familiar to them, provided them with plants and animals, revealed the nature of the land, and showed them how to make contact with the supernatural through offerings in certain places. They were told that it was their purpose to reproduce plants, animals, and people on the land bounded by the four sacred mountains (Mt. Taylor, San Francisco Peak, Hesperus Peak, and Blanco Peak, according to Wyman's *Blessingway*, 1970) and by the San Juan and Rio Grande rivers. They were told that as a people they were not to move beyond those boundaries. The supernaturals left them but said they would watch over them. If they did not care for the land, they would suffer. Thus the Navajo fear to leave the land. Furthermore, they have knowledge of this land, since their ceremonial practitioners tell them of the holy places where they may make offerings. Each family knows the locations in its area. When a person moves—say, to live with a spouse—the spouse's kin make the person familiar with the new land. If they move to some strange place, they are disoriented; they know nothing of how to use the land, religiously speaking. They fear for themselves, and they fear for the land, its plants, and its animals. In the Navajo view, the power of reproduction is embodied in nature: sky father and earth mother, male and female plants and animals, men and women, and the very country itself. The Lukachukai-Chuska range is male, moist with the power of rain; Black Mesa is part of a woman's figure, dry and, with its coal, having the character of the hearth, which is the woman's province. For the female figure to be half-severed from the Navajos threatens the reproductive power of nature itself.

If the Navajos lose the land the supernaturals told them to use, it is, they say, their end as a people. The present relocation is by the law of an external power, lacking both supernatural and traditional support. This power expels people from the land they know how to use through knowledge of livelihood, land, and ritual, and so it is unacceptable and incomprehensible to the Navajos. As one man said, "If you move us to the most beautiful mountains in the world, with plenty of rain, they will not be as beautiful to us as these little hills, where we make contact with nature and with our gods."

SUMMARY

Many relocatees blame their present predicament on the United States government. Many know that their ancestors lived in the former JUA before their captivity at Fort Sumner over a hundred years ago, and some know that their ancestors succeeded in avoiding the trip to Fort Sumner and stayed in the former JUA throughout the captivity. They believe that the Executive Order Reservation of 1882 was established for the Hopis by President Chester A. Arthur in disregard of the Navajos' own use of the land. While not challenging Hopi use of the area around their villages, the Navajos believe they have a historic right to the rest of the former JUA. The casual behavior of the Department of the Interior toward the Navajos in the former JUA encouraged that belief. The District Court acknowledged this in 1962 when it dealt with the land dispute: "While the Department of [the] Interior had not directly and officially settled Navajos in the 1882 lands, it had done so by implication, indirection, and neglect" (Navajo and Hopi Indian Relocation Commission 1978: 9).

Because of their special relationship to the land, Navajos see relocation as a threat to both their well-being and that of their children. Again and again, actual and potential relocatees stated their concern that relocation would sever their children from the land and in doing so cut them off from their Navajo heritage, a reasonable fear since participation in Navajo life and politics is dependent on being registered within a particular chapter.

Navajos living on the Hopi side of the partition line do not understand how Anglos and the government can relocate them from the only homes they know. Time and again, team members were told that relocation would not be necessary if only the Anglos knew what land meant to the people and if only they knew about the anguish that would result from compulsory removal. Though this belief is perhaps incomprehensible to highly mobile white Americans, it is hardly unique to the Navajos. Such an attitude has also been expressed by the Bikini islanders who have been subject to compulsory relocation by the United States government. As reported by Jerry Belcher in *The Los Angeles Times* (July 23, 1978) and reproduced in the *Congressional Record* (August 9, 1978), "there is among Micronesian peoples a profound, mystical attachment to the particular, tiny plots of land owned by their families or clans. In those islands, a man without land is no man."

CHAPTER 5

An Analysis of 1978 and 1979 Interviews with Navajo Relocatees and Potential Relocatees

Introduction

During December 1978 and January 1979 eighty-four interviews were carried out (see Table 1). Forty-eight involved compulsory relocatees, one of whom was only partially interviewed. Thirty-eight of these relocatees had been moved from the former JUA by the Relocation Commission. Of this group, thirty-four went to urban locales off the reservation (or to a rural setting within a few miles of the cities of Flagstaff, Gallup, or Winslow) and four moved to rural locales on the reservation. The other ten people interviewed were rural relocatees evicted from Black Mesa (three, two of whom also lived in the former JUA), District 6 (two), and the Navajo Indian Irrigation Project (five). The remaining thirty-six interviews were conducted among potential relocatees, all of whom still lived in that portion of the former JUA partitioned to the Hopis.

The information from these eighty-four interviews was coded by John Williamson, a graduate student in economics at the California Institute of Technology, who had no knowledge of the Navajo-Hopi land dispute prior to joining the study team in January 1979. Working separately, Williamson, another graduate student (Cynthia Carlson), and Thayer Scudder also divided forty-seven of the forty-eight compulsory relocatees into three general categories based on their personal evaluations of the information in the interviews. (See Appendixes 2 and 5 for a discussion of this methodology.) These categories concerned the

41

Table 1 Relocatee Breakdown

Category	Number	Reason for relocation
Compulsory relocatees		
Urban relocatees	34	Partition of the former JUA
Rural relocatees	14	Navajo Indian Irrigation Project—5 relocatees
		Partition of the former JUA—4 relocatees
		Coal mining on Black Mesa (and, in two cases, former JUA partition)— 3 relocatees
		Eviction from District 6— 2 relocatees
Total compulsory relocatees	48	
Potential relocatees	36	Partition of the former JUA
Total relocatees	84	

self-perceived adaptation to relocation (and relocation-associated problems) of the household head or spouse and his or her family. They consisted of "good copers" (17), "poor copers" (18), and those who fell in between (12). The *Statistical Package for the Social Sciences* (Nie et al. 1975) was used for the computer analysis of the data. The analysis in this chapter is based primarily on frequencies (percentages), i.e., the proportional response of interviewees to the same question.

One additional interview was mailed in by Kenneth Begishe after the computer analysis was completed. It is of special interest since the interviewee was a forty-six-year-old widow with no education who had relocated on her own initiative in August 1977 from the Hopi side of the former JUA after she heard that everyone would have to move. Staying within the same chapter, she sold her sheep and moved (prior to receiving any benefits from the Relocation Commission) to the customary use area of a relative. After ten months, she considered her relocation to be a failure and returned to her own home on the Hopi side of the partition line. Her interview will be analyzed in some detail since it pinpoints many of the problems caused by the compulsory relocation of Navajo women.

The results of our analysis are summarized in this chapter, and excerpts from selected interviews are presented in Appendix 3. We believe that the information given to us is substantially correct and that most interviewees tried very hard to express their feelings. In the few cases where we cross-checked information, we found it to be accurate. Cooperation with the interviewers was good. Most interviews lasted for one to two hours, although a number exceeded three hours. Of the eighty-four interviewees, only one refused to complete the interview, claiming that she was tired of being interviewed about relocation and wished to be left alone.

Compulsory Relocation

INTRODUCTION

Of the forty-eight households of compulsory relocatees in our sample, 20 percent have relocated within the past six months and 85 percent within the past two years. For at least 33 percent, this relocation was not the first time that they had been forced to move. Indeed, for four families this was their fourth compulsory relocation, and for two their third. This figure is disproportionately high since our sample includes a number of families that have been evicted from lands near the Hopi mesas on several occasions as a result of the expansion of District 6 to its present size. Nevertheless, the risk of multiple relocations is an ongoing threat to many Navajos.

As is the case elsewhere in the world, the majority of those who are forced to move resettle as close as possible to their former homes. That is why four families have had to move four times because of boundary readjustments around the current Hopi Reservation. Each time, they moved only a short distance—just beyond the new boundary. This problem of successive moves should not threaten future former JUA relocatees (except for those who cannot afford their new houses), but successive

43

dispossession does threaten Navajos who are being relocated elsewhere on the reservation and within adjacent areas of New Mexico. A number of Navajo Indian Irrigation Project (NIIP) relocatees had previously been forced to move because of the Navajo Coal Mine. Recently some have heard rumors that they may be moved again because their present homes are in the wrong place. In addition, some of those currently being evicted from Black Mesa and other mining lease areas may in fact be moving onto lands that will be mined in the future, thus subjecting them to another possible relocation.

We believe that a single agency within the Navajo tribal administration should be responsible for all Navajos threatened by compulsory relocation, whether through legal action, highway construction, mining, agricultural development, or other causes. Such an agency should attempt to reduce the compulsory relocation of Navajo households to the absolute minimum, both by assessing the relocation implications of different options and the future relocation risks in areas to which relocatees wish to move.

The evidence from our interviews with the forty-eight respondents supports the conclusion that Navajo relocatees, like other low-income rural populations with strong ties to the land, find compulsory relocation a very stressful experience during the transition period. Topper's data and the high death rate among District 6 relocatees, as well as the interview data, suggest that relocation stress among former JUA relocatees will exceed that of most other populations of relocatees that have been studied. One reason for this has already been mentioned: the very strong attachment of Navajos to the land and especially to the customary use area in which they have grown up. A second reason may well relate to a general insecurity over tenure to that land. Stories passed down through several generations have given all Navajos vivid images of the "Long Walk" to Fort Sumner in 1864, a compulsory relocation that involved most of the tribe. In the past forty years, some Navajos have been forced to move for a variety of reasons; those who have not are still aware of such moves. They love their land; they are identified with it; and yet they know that the United States government and the tribal administration not only have the authority to move them but all too frequently use that authority. It is because of this general insecurity, compounded by the development freeze in the former JUA and the difficulty of obtaining homesite leases on the reservation, that some urban relocatees actually decided to move to town rather than hold out or seek on-reservation relocation. Some Navajo relocatees from the former JUA told us that they moved because past United States government intervention made it too difficult to stay. Better to own a house and a small plot in town, several educated interviewees reported, than to have a sixty-five year lease to a piece of land in the reservation which you know belongs to your family but which you also know can be taken from you at any time.

Those Navajos most seriously affected by compulsory relocation are older men and adult women of any age. We have already mentioned the life-threatening implications of relocation for the elderly. We also believe that women are more threatened than men because it is mainly through women that land and the basis of a Navajo identity are passed on to succeeding generations. This concern was made explicit by the NIIP relocatees, all five of whom were women who had been moved from their customary use areas to new holdings less than one acre in size. All were "poor copers."

One of these five said, "They should give us additional land for my children. . . . I [can] not plan ahead for my children anymore. I am afraid that they will just scatter when they get older." Another reported, "Yes, we do worry [about our children], because we have only one acre of land, and our children have no place to live when they get older." Still another declared, "It seems like this is the end for us here. Our future plan for our children is disrupted. Our children were not considered in the relocation plan." The fourth and fifth women also voiced similar concerns.

Particularly instructive is Begishe's interview with a forty-six-year-old widow who, upon being told she would soon have to relocate, sold all her sheep and moved to a relative's land, only to abandon her "experiment" ten months later in order to return home to the Hopi side of the partition line. On her relative's land some hosts spoke to her with harsh words:

> "You are not a local resident," I was told. . . . I was sick throughout the year at the place of relocation. Thus I have come to the conclusion that I was dying because I missed my land so much. Thus, accordingly, I discovered that a person can or will die of loneliness if he or she is removed from his or her land. . . . After I relocated I kept dreaming of walking along on the land that I left; this haunted me continually. Thus, I came to realize, the same land that I left was grieving me to death. And then as a result of selling all my livestock, my [three unmarried] children hungered for mutton as they hopelessly look[ed] around. My children said, "We now realize that it is not good to live without sheep." I had realized myself that it is very lonely without any sheep, not even a hoofprint of one was around. . . . Thus that was the main reason why I was dying of loneliness a year ago. I really tried hard to [find] something to take the place of . . . having sheep. Now I realize that there is nothing to take its place. . . . When there are no sheep at home there is no reason to stay home or return home. . . . When one sells all of his sheep one becomes idle because there is nothing to do at home. When one sells all of his sheep, one will begin to feel useless. . . . When I sold all of my sheep, all of my future planning was gone. . . . When I sold all of my sheep, all of my children became uninterested in our home. When I sold all of my sheep, all of my children don't stay at home anymore. . . . When one has livestock the children will come back from school to work on different things at home. After we sold all our sheep everything else became uninteresting. When there are no sheep, one's home no longer is a real home. Now that we don't have any more sheep, we are continually in need. . . . My sheep were my only security. . . . And then, from the top of Black Mesa, my mother she asked me to come back; thus we went back and all of my sickness left. And I became as healthy as before, as I went long distances herding [my mother's] sheep— which I never did before. . . . Even though I moved back now, it is still frustrating without [any] sheep. There are the empty sheep corral[s]. As I look at [them], I still get depressed. I go back to those empty corrals and grieve with sorrow.

INTERVIEWEE CHARACTERISTICS

Of the forty-eight relocatees interviewed, approximately two-thirds were household heads; the others were the spouses of household heads. Frequently both were present and elaborated on each other's answers. While this had the advantage of expanding the information given and increasing the number of respondents, in some cases the interviewer forgot to specify who was talking, making cross-tabulations on the basis of sex more difficult. Women predominated in the sample: twenty-six women to twenty-two men. Of these interviewees, 75 percent were married, 10 percent widowed, 8 percent divorced, and 4 percent separated.

Age categories are shown in Table 2. All but one of those twenty-nine and younger were urban relocatees from the former JUA, a fact that points up one of a number of ways in which the initial former JUA relocatees can be expected to vary from those still to move. Again, because of the relative youth of the sample, the average household size (6.3 persons, with 5.4 living at home) was also smaller than that within the reservation or the former JUA. Current residence is shown in Table 3; the Flagstaff and St. Johns relocatees are all from the former JUA.

The interviewees belonged to fourteen chapters, with the largest number coming from Tolani Lake (34 percent), followed

Table 2   Age of Compulsory Relocatees

Age	Number of interviewees	Adjusted percentage	Accumulative adjusted percentage
20–29 Years	17	36.2	36.2
30–39 Years	9	19.1	55.3
40–49 Years	11	23.4	78.7
50–59 Years	5	10.65	89.4
60 Years and over	5	10.65	100.0
Unknown	1	—	
Total	48	100.00	

Table 3   Current Residences of Compulsory
Relocatees

Location	Number of interviewees
Chinle	1
Flagstaff	21
Forest Lake	2
Gallup	2
Kayenta	1
St. Johns	5
Teesto	2
Tolani Lake	2
Tuba City	1
Upper Fruitland	4
White Cone	1
Winslow	2
Other on Reservation	4
Total	48

by Coal Mine Mesa (17 percent), Teesto (13 percent), and Upper Fruitland (8 percent). Tolani Lake predominates simply because a disproportionate number of the first former JUA relocatees come from that chapter—especially the Sand Springs area, from which a number of related families have moved. Most continue to vote in chapter elections (approximately 80 percent voted in 1978) and participate in religious activities.

Table 4 shows the educational levels of interviewees and their spouses. What elevates these levels well above those for the reservation as a whole is the generally superior education of the first urban relocatees from the former JUA; all other relocatees have more typical educational backgrounds. Notwithstanding these relatively high levels of education, and notwithstanding the fact that approximately two-thirds of the former JUA urban relocatees were living in town prior to their resettlement by the Relocation Commission, 53 percent of the interviewees were unemployed (in terms of wage labor) at the time of the interview, as were 49 percent of the spouses. The unemployment rate among the men (whether household head or spouse) was lower than that of the women. Approximately 20 percent of the interviewees were receiving welfare.

In spite of the disproportionate number of young, well-educated people in our sample who had jobs and who had lived in town previous to relocation, 27 percent replied "none" when asked to list the positive aspects of relocation. Another 19 percent gave the same answer but then referred during subsequent questioning to such beneficial aspects as better and closer schooling for children, easier access to work, and improved housing. Forty-eight percent considered the family worse off financially since resettlement, while 35 percent saw an improvement in their financial position. The remainder saw no major change one way or the other.

In discussing the negative aspects of relocation (a question that followed that dealing with positive aspects), the overwhelming majority stressed problems associated with the loss of their customary use area (Table 5). A still prevalent Navajo custom is for parents to bury the navel cord of their children near a dwelling place on their land. This act symbolizes the child's permanent association with that site by ensuring that the person's mind will always return there. When interviewees were asked if their parents had so buried their navel cords, 91 percent

Table 4   Education of Compulsory Relocatees

Years of education	Interviewee		Spouse	
	Number	Adjusted frequency	Number	Adjusted frequency
None	10	20.8	7	18.9
1–4	5	10.4	3	8.2
5–8	6	12.5	5	13.5
9–12	21	43.8	15	40.5
13 or more	6	12.5	7	18.9
Unknown	—	—	3	—
Total	48	100.0	40*	100.0

*This figure is higher than the number of current spouses since some respondents gave educational status data for a deceased or divorced spouse.

49

Table 5   Negative Aspects of Relocation

Category*	Number of interviewees	Adjusted percentage
Aspects associated with loss of customary use area		
Fear loss of Navajo identity	17	36.2
Separation from land and stock	10	21.2
No land for children	2	4.3
Total	29	61.7
Aspects associated with relocation area		
Too expensive	4	8.5
Too far from Indian Health Service	1	2.1
Total	5	10.6
Combination of above aspects	11	23.4
None	2	4.3
No answer given	1	—
Total	48	100.0

*Wherever possible an attempt was made to isolate the most important single aspect, even though several were mentioned.

of the forty-five who replied to this question answered in the affirmative. When those respondents were asked if their mind kept returning to that place, 90 percent said yes. In some cases, the navel cord had been buried in the sheep corral, hence "tying" the person to sheep herding. In the words of one woman, "I was told that my navel cord was put in a sheep corral, so my mind is made up to have sheep all my life." When subsequently asked how she felt about leaving the place where her navel cord was buried she replied, "I am grieving for my sheep," again showing the strong associations involved.

As we have said throughout this study, a person's land and sheep have a symbolic importance that transcends their economic value. Indeed, their sociocultural value is such that they are an intricate part of a person's identity. The same applies to the political role of land in Navajo society. As Philip Reno states (1978), "Young people growing into maturity find their social status and their role in tribal politics based on their home community. If they relocate [compulsorily] they cannot accumulate community status and political roles in a new community."

When interviewees were asked what they missed most since their relocation, land and/or livestock took precedence in over 90 percent of the answers. Although 80 percent no longer have any livestock today because of destocking and relocation, half of the forty-six people who answered this question also volunteered the information that they did have animals in the past. The combined loss of both land and stock is a very heavy burden to bear and can be expected to threaten the health of a significant number of those involved.

Although the interviewees were most concerned about the loss of their customary use areas, 76 percent claimed to have special financial problems since relocation. Although we would expect many Navajos to have financial problems (regardless of whether or not they were relocatees) simply because their unemployment rate is so high, relocatees tend to have two additional problems. The first, shared with all former JUA residents, is loss of livestock; as we have seen, at one time livestock provided about 25 percent of the former JUA household's income. The second problem is presented by the increased costs of improved housing.

Throughout the world, compulsory relocation tends to be associated with improved housing for the relocatees. This is a plus that applies to most former JUA relocatees, though not necessarily to other Navajo relocatees. Among thirty-three former JUA urban relocatees on whom relevant information was gathered, 35 percent had positive or very positive reactions to their housing as opposed to 27 percent with negative or very negative reactions; the remainder had mixed reactions.

However, improved housing is costly to maintain. It also tends to be electrified, so that for the first time many Navajo relocatees are paying substantial utility bills, which even employed Navajos are finding hard to afford. As for those currently unemployed, it is doubtful that they will be able to pay for the utility, maintenance and, in town, tax and insurance costs of their new houses, even though most are mortgage-free. Several urban relocatees already are trying to sell their houses, and a few others in our sample intend to. We expect their number to increase in the years ahead.

The problem of not being able to afford new housing is not unique to the Navajos. Rather, it is a characteristic of urban redevelopment throughout the United States. The problem lies with the Uniform Relocation Act of 1970. This act stipulates that relocatees who move from areas in which federal funds are used must be provided with decent, safe, and sanitary replacement housing. However, the act does not deal with the problem of how relocatees can afford that housing. Since no support, let alone funds, is provided for economic development associated with relocation, many of the poorer relocatees find that they cannot afford their new quarters—so they move out or are forced to cut down on other essential expenditures. We expect this problem to continue to be a major one for former JUA relocatees who are unemployed, seasonally employed, or employed as unskilled workers on low salaries. Although it will affect both rural and urban relocatees, this problem will be especially serious among the latter unless future Navajo relocation is linked more directly with a program to improve job skills and provide more employment opportunities.

The major benefit associated with Navajo relocation is closer and/or improved access to schools. The majority of relocatees believe that their children like their schools and that they are doing well. When asked in what way their children benefited from relocation, the most common response (46 percent of the total) was that they were better off because they were closer to schools. For the most part, this meant that children could now attend local public schools as day students rather than board out at distant BIA and other schools. While they have new types of worries, Navajo parents were delighted to have their children around; this points up the hardship that the freeze on school construction in their former location imposed upon them. Some of the Navajo parents complained of instances of discrimination, but they also appeared to be glad to have their children in public as opposed to BIA schools. This, however, may be more a commentary on the remoteness of the latter than on their quality.

Whenever relocation is required, every effort should be made to provide the best possible education for the children of relocatees so as to increase their chances of finding future employment. Although one-third of the interviewees stated that relocation had not improved the lot of their children, 66 percent felt that relocation had not worsened their children's lot in any way. Forty percent of the relocatees had no special worries about their children since removal. This response is encouraging. While it does not mean that children are not facing special problems (after all, one-third of the interviewees stated or implied that their children were now worse off), it does show that, in general, parents perceive relocation as being less stressful for their children than for themselves and for their older dependents.

Compulsory relocatees belonged to a variety of religions: 35 percent categorized themselves as Protestants, 18 percent as members of the Native American Church (NAC), 13 percent as both NAC members and followers of traditional Navajo beliefs, and 8 percent as traditional Navajo believers. Relocation is often associated with a temporary reduction in religious activities, but we know relatively little about the response of Navajo relocatees in this regard. We do know, however, that most informants agreed that Navajo ceremonials could not be held in locations like downtown Flagstaff or Gallup, which lie outside the boundaries of the four sacred mountains. Some informants also claimed that such ceremonies could not be held in houses built of stone or cinder block, regardless of their location—though a few medicine men told us that this was not necessarily true. The situation may well vary from one ceremony to another or from one medicine man to another since some rural relocatees told us that they had held traditional Navajo ceremonies in their new cinder block houses, while another stated that he had not been able to hold such a ceremony, a situation that obviously concerned him. Urban relocatees living outside the boundaries of Navajo land who wished to hold such ceremonies sought out the hogans of rural relatives. Though obviously an inconvenience was involved, we do not know how serious this problem will become, both as time goes by and as more and more relatives leave the former JUA.

Relocatees were also asked if their experiences had influenced the relocation plans of relatives still living on the Hopi side of the partition line. In their answers, relocatees not only stated their belief that the majority of their relatives did not plan to move but also that the relocatees' own experiences had increased the proportion that did not plan to move. Illustrated in Table 6, these data are one reason why we do not expect the number of relocatees currently living in the former JUA (as opposed to those living outside the former JUA who can be expected to apply for

Table 6   Effect of the Relocatees' Experiences on the Relocation Plans of Relatives Currently Resident on the Hopi Side of the Former JUA

Effect	Number of interviewees	Adjusted percentage
NO EFFECT: Relatives didn't intent to move before and still do not intend to move.	13	48.2
NO EFFECT: Relatives planned to move before and still plan to move.	7	25.9
YES EFFECT: Relocatee experiences have changed relatives' plans; now they do not intend to move.	3	11.1
YES EFFECT: Relocatee experiences have changed relatives' plans; now they plan to relocate on rather than off the reservation.	2	7.4
YES EFFECT: Relocatee experiences have caused relatives to postpone making a relocation decision.	1	3.7
OTHER	1	3.7
QUESTION INAPPLICABLE (no relatives on Hopi side of partition line; relatives have already relocated; etc.)	18	—
INSUFFICIENT DATA TO CODE	3	—
Total	48	100.0

benefits under the new eligibility criteria) to increase significantly in the near future unless new and unexpected circumstances emerge.

This study is especially concerned with factors that account for how well respondents cope with relocation. It is reasonable to expect that the age, sex, education, place of relocation, and employment of the compulsory relocatees in the sample would affect their adjustment to relocation. Other variables might be considered, but only these are explored here. For a satisfactory analysis of the relationship of each of these variables to overall adjustment, a multivariate approach is necessary. The results of the analysis are summarized here. More detail is provided in Appendix 4, where a matrix of gamma scores, a smallest-space analysis, and the systematic application of controls are used to arrive at the conclusions that are presented in this chapter. In what follows, statements about statistical relationships are kept separate from inferences based both on the statistics and on a knowledge of Navajo culture and the situation of relocatees.

In the general Navajo population and among the relocatees interviewed, there is a marked negative relationship between age and education. Older people had far fewer opportunities to receive a usable amount of education when they were growing up. The level of education is also strongly and positively associated with the place of relocation: the more educated have been relocated to urban settings, the less educated to rural ones. The judgment of people's overall adjustment to relocation is strongly associated with their relocation site: rural relocatees are almost all judged to have serious adjustment problems, while urban relocatees have proportionately fewer. (See Appendix 2 for the method of making the judgment of overall adjustment.) It is inferred that the effect of the relocation site does not result from Navajo preference for urban sites—indeed, many now in an urban setting would prefer to be back on the reservation. Rather, the relationship between urban relocation and better overall adjustment results from the inadequate conditions of rural relocation, where there are almost no jobs, where most relocatees cannot carry on traditional pastoral activities (because

55

they cannot get permission to move their stock to the relocation site), and where other grave problems may confront them.

One of the most important findings is that the sex of the respondent exerts a fairly strong effect on the individual's adjustment, one that is not mediated by age, education, place of relocation, or employment status. That is, Navajo women are judged to have more serious adjustment problems than men. It is inferred that the reason for this is that women suffer a special deprivation through relocation, almost regardless of where they go. They are the normal channels for transmitting rights in land to their children, especially to their daughters. Removed from their homeland and unable to return to it, they feel a special sense of loss.

One might expect that employment status would have a marked effect on adjustment. It does not. Rather, employment is affected by the relocation site—few rural respondents are employed. A special analysis of employment that takes into account whether a married respondent's spouse is employed improved the association between employment and adjustment, but without altering the basic relationship of the variables.

It is a matter of some importance that the analysis distinguishes two sets of variables that account for adjustment: (1) an interrelated set that comprises age, education, and place of relocation; and (2) the sex of the respondent. Methodologically, multivariate analysis is a crucial tool for relocation studies. Empirically, the findings about the serious problems experienced by female Navajo relocatees are of special value in considering the impact of relocation on Navajos. The loss experienced by relocated women cannot, it seems, be compensated for by economic advantages, improved housing, or monetary payments.

Urban Relocatees from the Former Joint Use Area

Thirty-four interviews were carried out (of which one was incomplete) among former JUA urban relocatees, all of whom moved under the auspices of the Navajo and Hopi Indian Relocation Commission. Table 7 shows their current location as well as that of all relocatees moved by the Relocation Commission prior to the beginning of our study in December 1978. During our brief survey we were able to interview 59 percent of all the relocatees moved by the Relocation Commission, including all the rural relocatees and 57 percent of the urban relocatees. In this section, we are concerned only with the latter.

The urban relocatees differ in a number of major ways from the much larger number of former JUA Navajos who have yet to relocate. They are younger, better educated, and have a higher employment rate—all characteristics associated with a greater capacity to adjust to compulsory relocation. Furthermore, at the time of their relocation two-thirds of the interviewees were already living in town rather than on the reservation. For these people, relocation came at a time when they had already left the reservation to find work or to pursue higher education. While

Table 7   Current Location of Former JUA Relocatees Moved by the Relocation Commission Through 1978

Location	Number of relocatees moved by Relocation Commission	Number of Relocation Commission relocatees interviewed
Flagstaff	36	23
Winslow	7	2
St. Johns	5	4
Gallup	3	3*
Phoenix	2	0
Page	1	1
Other off-reservation urban locales	6	1
Subtotal: Urban relocatees	60	34
On-reservation rural relocatees	4	4
Total relocatees	64	38

*One incomplete.

they maintained close ties with their customary use areas, and have suffered stress as a result of partition, some have benefited from relocation in a number of ways. In particular, they have been able to purchase a house outright, which they otherwise would not have been able to do. This is a major benefit, one that will now apply to other skilled and employed Navajos currently living and working off the reservation who will qualify for relocation benefits under the new eligibility criteria. It is important to emphasize, however, that the number of such household heads is relatively small. The majority of potential relocatees still living in the former JUA are older and less well-educated, with a higher unemployment rate.

Table 8 compares the ages of household heads who have relocated to town with those still resident in the former JUA and includes information on those living on both the Navajo and Hopi sides of the partition line. The data clearly show the age differential between the two populations: 82 percent of the former JUA household heads are forty or older, as opposed to only 23 percent of the urban relocatees. The data also suggest that middle-aged household heads are holding back from relocating. Widowed elderly parents, on the other hand, are more apt to join their relocated children, both out of loneliness and fear of being left alone on the reservation.

Table 9 compares the educational levels of urban relocatees with heads of households still resident in the former JUA. Information on the first group came from the thirty-four interviewees, 30 percent of whom were spouses of household heads. While the information is not exactly comparable, especially since younger women have a higher level of education than men, the contrast between the two populations is striking. Two-thirds of the urban relocatees have had at least some high school education, while only 12 percent of those still resident in the former JUA have attained that level. Since "youth" and "nine or more years of education" are the most important indicators (other than male sex) of capacity to cope with compulsory relocation, the low educational levels and higher ages of those who live on the Hopi side of the former JUA can be expected to

Table 8 Age Distribution of Household Heads

	Urban relocatees*			Former JUA residents†		
Age range	Number	Adjusted percentage	Accumulative percentage	Number	Adjusted percentage	Accumulative percentage
20–29	29	46	46	7	5	5
30–39	20	31	77	19	13	18
40–49	6	9	86	38	26	44
50–59	3	5	91	32	22	66
60 and over	6	9	100	50	34	100
Total	64	100.0		146	100.0	

*From the Navajo and Hopi Indian Relocation Commission's Interim Progress Report (1978: 148); data include four rural relocatees.
†Information provided by John Wood.

Table 9 Educational Levels of Urban Relocatee Household Heads or Their Spouses and Heads of Household Still Resident in the Former JUA

	Urban relocatees			Former JUA residents*		
Years of education	Number	Adjusted percentage	Accumulative percentage	Number	Adjusted percentage	Accumulative percentage
None	4	11.8	11.8	85	58	58
1–4	1	2.9	14.7	20	14	72
5–8	4	11.8	26.5	24	16	88
9–12	19	55.9	82.4	16	11	99
13 and over	6	17.6	100.0	1	1	100
Total	34	100.0		146	100.0	

*Information provided by John Wood.

increase the proportion of future relocatees with serious adjustment problems.

As for employment, 57 percent of the interviewees were employed versus only 36 percent of household heads still resident within the former JUA. In this regard, the contrast is even more striking than the figures suggest, since urban interviewees who are female spouses had a higher unemployment rate than their husbands. (The unemployment rate among female interviewees was 47 percent versus 41 percent for men, although some of the latter were only seasonally unemployed.)

Urban interviewees scored much higher than the majority of Navajo heads of households still living on the Hopi side of the partition line in regard to attributes that correlate with an increased capability to cope with compulsory relocation. However, only 46 percent of the thirty-three interviewees on whom information was collected were classified as "good copers." Thirty-three percent were termed "mixed copers" and 21 percent "poor copers." Among women, only one-fourth were "good copers," while another one-fourth were "poor copers." Even employment did not raise the proportion of "good copers" over 50 percent, since 44 percent of those who were employed were "mixed copers" and 11 percent "poor copers." None of the five interviewees who were on welfare was adjusting well. The only situation (aside from male sex) in which "good copers" were in the majority among urban relocatees occurred when those involved either had nine or more years of education or were between twenty and twenty-nine. In this case, youth also correlated with a higher educational level.

Although 44 percent of the urban relocatees considered themselves better off financially since relocation, 66 percent believed that they had serious financial problems—including 50 percent of those who were employed. We wish to consider this problem in some detail since it illustrates how even relatively young and educated Navajos are having difficulties as urban-dwelling homeowners.

Within the former JUA, the large majority of people haul water and wood to homes that are not electrified. They build and maintain their houses themselves or get help from local workers either by hiring them or through home improvement funds. No taxes are paid, and we suspect that very few people have homeowners' insurance policies. Although Navajos moving to town know that the situation there is very different, most are unprepared for the new responsibilities and expenses that fall upon them when they use relocation benefits to purchase a house (because of less rapid depreciation and other factors, the Relocation Commission recommends that relocatees buy houses rather than mobile homes). As a result, it is not surprising that over 70 percent of the interviewees talked about housing problems, and the large majority of these related to the expenses involved. In stressing this point we are not suggesting that Navajos should be discouraged from becoming homeowners (36 percent felt positive about their housing and 27 percent noted no housing problems). Rather, we wish to make the point that relocatees need much more thorough counseling before and after relocating. In other words, if relocation continues, the Relocation Commission should be given the authority and the funds either to execute or coordinate a much-improved program in which financial counseling and home maintenance are emphasized.

At least ten of the thirty-three urban relocatees on whom we have information make over $1,000 per month, but the most common salary range is $500 to $600 per month. Although taxes and insurance usually are prepaid during the first year from benefits and the large majority of houses are purchased clear of mortgage, most relocatees spend their $5,000 incentive allowance during the first twelve months (especially on furniture or a pickup truck) so that thereafter they are entirely dependent on their salaries or, if they are unemployed, on general assistance and other benefits. As owners of houses that are usually valued at over $30,000, those making $7,200 or less per year can expect to have serious problems in paying utility, insurance, and tax bills, not to mention the special costs associated with such housing mishaps as clogged plumbing and burst pipes. Utilities often run over $30 per month, while annual taxes and insurance each tend to exceed $200 per year. Lower-income interviewees found such bills very difficult to pay. One twenty-seven-year-old man whose salary was $600 per month reported that he was hard pressed to pay property taxes of $229 per annum; indeed, he feared that he might lose his house. Of course, the situation is much more serious among the unemployed. One woman had let her insurance lapse because she couldn't afford it. However, her problems, like those of others, extended beyond house expenses to all expenses. The following examples make this plain: "We seldom have enough money for anything, especially utility bills, food, clothes, extras." "We don't have enough income to keep up with our bills. Our income of $375 [per month from Aid for Dependent Children, etc.] barely covers our utilities and payments for the furniture we bought when we moved here." "Our income does not cover all our expenses, especially food costs." "Money barely covers the necessities; none left over for clothes or meat. I am presently applying for food stamps." Although the Relocation Commission has been trying to resolve the problem, some of the unemployed have not been able to receive the full assistance to which they are entitled since state and other agencies have yet to understand that their incentive allowances and other relocation benefits are tax-exempt.

Even Navajos with higher salaries have problems, either because they do not know how to properly budget their income or because their lack of experience with housing leads to expensive repairs. For example, two families, trying to lower heating costs while absent on short visits, turned their thermostats so low during the severe cold spell in December 1978 that their pipes burst, flooding their homes. Several others took out mortgages so that they could purchase additional land and are now struggling with monthly payments of between $200 and $300. Others, faced with a variety of debts, have consolidated them by taking out a single loan of $10,000 to $15,000 with monthly payments of $196 to $256. In such cases, it is exceedingly unlikely that these individuals have the background to shop around for the best deal, especially since some were not even aware that significant differences existed in interest rates between banks and finance companies.

Because of inexperience, urban relocatees are also having problems with the routine running of household appliances and with house care. When the elderly and children are unaccustomed to using indoor plumbing, the family may suffer from stopped-up toilets, sewer lines, and septic tanks. A mother and daughter living together stated that they did not know how to care for their appliances or their house; the elderly mother did not know how to operate the stove or the thermostat while her daughter was at work. A fifty-six-year-old man did not know how to operate his new self-cleaning oven. Unless people are taught how to care for their homes, they will experience the stress caused by frequent breakdowns and costly repairs, and the value of their homes will depreciate more rapidly. Such problems are one reason why the Relocation Commission is increasingly urging elderly and uneducated Navajos to relocate on the reservation. However, rural relocatees in improved housing on the reservation will still need instruction in how to care for their homes. One head of a household (a woman) living in on-reservation improved housing financed by the Relocation Commission did not know how to lock the front door of her home, while another woman was afraid when pots boiled over on her gas stove.

Although they are coping better than other Navajo relocatees, primarily because of their youth and better education, urban relocatees strongly resent being required to leave the former JUA. When asked why they first moved to town, no relocatees phrased their answer in terms of the positive drawing power of town employment or town facilities. Rather, of the thirty-three who gave answers, 52 percent replied that they came because they could not make a living on the reservation, while 39 percent referred to the freeze on new housing construction. Another 6 percent said they moved because of rumors and the belief that the housing situation in town would deteriorate if they delayed. Three percent (one family) noted that they would only get help if they left. Like other relocatees, the large majority of urban interviewees (79 percent) stated that their navel cords were buried within a customary use area, and that their minds kept returning to that location. Fifty-five percent were also concerned about the fate of Navajo graves after the people depart from the Hopi side of the partition line. They fear both neglect and desecration of gravesites; a few referred to cases in which Hopis allegedly removed poles from burial sites. As for the negative aspects of relocation, the majority—like other relocatees—stressed loss of land, livestock, and/or their Navajo identity, with only two (6 percent) stating that relocation involved no negative aspects. Thirty-six percent said there were no positive aspects to relocation, although over half of these subsequently qualified their answers by mentioning such benefits as closer and better schooling for children, closer work, and improved housing.

Generally speaking, urban relocatees are less likely to become involved in community and state activities than to maintain their involvement in reservation life. Thus, whereas 73 percent voted in the 1978 tribal elections, only 42 percent are registered to vote in state elections. When asked whether they had joined any voluntary association (other than a church) since coming to town, 88 percent replied in the negative. Though slightly over 50 percent claimed to be Christians (Christian identification is much higher among the better-educated urban relocatees than among rural relocatees), those who had actually attended church since relocating in town were only about half that number.

In their January 1979 *Program Update and Report*, the staff of the Navajo and Hopi Indian Relocation Commission stated that they continue to be "extremely concerned over the adjustment of approximately 25 percent of the families that have moved off-reservation." This concern is entirely legitimate. Although some younger men are involved, elderly men and female relocatees find town relocation particularly difficult. Though much of the problem is related to compulsory removal from their homes—rather than town versus on-reservation relocation—housing expenses are higher in town while benefits, especially for the unemployed, are less. There is neither an Indian Health Service

(IHS) hospital nor an IHS clinic in Flagstaff, despite the fact that this is where most potential relocatees with an urban preference wish to move; the IHS hospital in Winslow has been downgraded to a clinic. As a result, Navajos needing hospitalization, emergency, or other medical services must use a private facility or travel to the IHS hospital in Tuba City. The medical fees and transportation costs involved in either option are costly.

Rural Relocatees

INTRODUCTION

Fourteen interviews were carried out among rural relocatees who were required to leave their customary use areas. Four had relocated from the former JUA since 1978, five had relocated in connection with the Navajo Indian Irrigation Project, two were District 6 relocatees, and three were Black Mesa (Peabody Coal Lease) relocatees (two of whom were also former JUA relocatees). For reasons that will be explained below, these fourteen relocatees were having a much harder time with removal than the urban relocatees. Only two were classified as "good copers" and only one as a "mixed coper." The other eleven (79 percent of the total) were classified as "poor copers."

Only 15 percent of the urban relocatees saw no positive aspects of relocation, but a majority of the rural relocatees (57 percent) felt that way. As with all compulsory relocatees, they were most concerned about loss of land, livestock, and their Navajo identity. Although they were relocated on the reservation, 50 percent singled out their fear that their Navajo identity might be lost as the worst aspect of removal, clearly illustrating the close association between a person's well-being and living in his or her customary use area. Of the rural relocatees, 82 percent expressed concern over leaving behind ancestral burial sites; only 55 percent of the urban relocatees felt this same concern.

All of the rural relocatees had special financial problems since relocation (versus 66 percent of the urban relocatees). Eighty-six percent (versus 31 percent) considered themselves worse off

65

financially. They were also more concerned about problem drinking in their families (35 percent versus 13 percent), while their opinions about their current housing were much more negative than was the case with urban interviewees. While only 6 percent of the latter had very negative opinions about their housing, 50 percent of the rural relocatees felt that way. Indeed, none had positive feelings (let alone very positive feelings) about resettlement housing. In contrast, 36 percent of the urban relocatees felt positively about their homes. Rural relocatees were also more concerned about their children than urban relocatees. While 82 percent of the urban relocatees did not think that conditions were worse in any way for their children since relocation, only 31 percent of the rural relocatees felt that way.

This major contrast between rural and urban relocatees occurs not because rural relocation is more difficult or stressful for Navajos than urban relocation; on the contrary, the opposite is the case. Rather, the difference can be attributed to a number of factors, of which the following three are probably the most important: (1) The rural relocatees score much lower than the urban relocatees on characteristics that correlate with increased capability to cope with compulsory relocation. As a population, they contain a higher proportion of women. They are also older and less well-educated, and they have a higher unemployment rate. (2) On the whole, they were relocated at an earlier date. As a result, they have had more time to consider and suffer the disadvantages of compulsory relocation, especially as they relate to their children's landlessness. (3) With the exception of four out of the six rural relocatees from the former JUA, they also received fewer benefits from the relocating agency than did the urban relocatees.

COPING CHARACTERISTICS

While 47 percent of the urban relocatees were women, the percentage among the rural relocatees was 71 percent. The average age of urban relocatees was thirty-seven years, as opposed to forty-five for the rural relocatees. The educational qualifications of the two populations are compared in Table 10. Of the rural relocatees, 71 percent had less than five years of education, versus only 15 percent of the urban relocatees. We have already noted that some high school or higher education correlates with increased ability to cope with compulsory relocation. While 73 percent of the urban relocatees fell into this category, only 14 percent (two) of the rural relocatees did, and neither of these had gone beyond high school. As for employment, only 23 percent of the rural interviewees were employed, versus 56 percent of the urban interviewees.

DATE OF REMOVAL

While all but one of the urban relocatees have been moved since the beginning of 1977, eight (57 percent) of the rural relocatees were removed before that date. Three of these (21 percent) moved in 1972. They have had longer to think about the implications of removal for themselves and their families and to dwell upon (and in some cases magnify) the hardships and injustices they believe they have suffered. In particular, they have begun to see more clearly the implications of compulsory relocation for their dependent children, for whom there will be no relocation benefits in the form of housing and a small plot of land when they mature and marry. What will happen to them? Obviously, they will scatter, since the relocatees have insufficient land upon which to build. Will they also become depressed, start drinking, and get into trouble? These are the kinds of worries that are burdening rural relocatees, especially the five NIIP relocatees, all of whom, as previously mentioned, are very concerned about the landlessness of their dependent children.

BENEFITS

We have already emphasized the fact that relocation benefits within the United States do not compare favorably with those in many other countries since they do not include community services and economic assistance for the relocatees.

Table 10 Educational Levels of Rural and Urban Relocatee Interviewees

Years of education	Rural relocatees			Urban relocatees		
	Number	Adjusted percentage	Accumulative percentage	Number	Adjusted percentage	Accumulative percentage
None	6	42.9	42.9	4	11.8	11.8
1–4	4	28.5	71.4	1	2.9	14.7
5–8	2	14.3	85.7	4	11.8	26.5
9–12	2	14.3	100.0	19	55.9	82.4
13 and over	0	—	100.0	6	17.6	100.0
Total	14	100.0		34	100.0	

Nevertheless, the benefits contained within Public Law 93–531 are good by United States standards. In addition to adequate housing benefits and reimbursement of moving expenses, there is an incentive allowance of $5,000 per family for those who move either before or within one year of the approval by Congress of the relocation plan. The intent of Congress is also to provide community facilities—a major step in the right direction, although no funds have yet been allocated for that purpose. In contrast, the benefits provided to District 6, Black Mesa (Peabody Coal Leases), and NIIP relocatees are lower. The District 6 situation is the worst, followed by Black Mesa and NIIP.

District 6 Relocation. Following the enlargement of the Hopi Reservation (District 6) to its present size in 1943, over 100 Navajo families were moved out. However, at least fifteen families stayed on in Echo Canyon, where they had customary use areas and grazing permits. Isolated from other Navajos, they belonged to two extended families that closely intermarried and formed an isolated and traditionally oriented group. When these families were told to move by the United States District Court in 1966, they appealed the decision. On October 10, 1972, the Supreme Court refused to review the February 18, 1972 decision of the Court of Appeals for the Ninth Circuit, which reaffirmed the eviction. With only thirty days notice, all fifteen families were compulsorily relocated on November 10. The members of at least one family watched their home go up in smoke as they left. It was set on fire, they claimed, by the Hopis and their range riders.

The relocation of these fifteen District 6 families was co-ordinated by the Navajo-Hopi Land Dispute Commission. Although the Commission had established that most if not all of the families had relatives who were willing to provide land for homesite leases (but not for livestock), these relatives lived within the former JUA. This meant, of course, that movement to relatives' land was not possible since the freeze prohibited the construction of new housing to accommodate them. As a result, the tribe took over and relocated them and their livestock in temporary quarters (house trailers) on the Navajo Tribal Fair Grounds in Window Rock. That night it snowed. Not all the gas lines for heating and cooking had been connected up, and some of the elderly people and the children had to be transported to the Fort Defiance Indian Hospital for observation. Forty days later, Joe Kabinto, the patriarch of the families, died. He was the first of nine adults (nearly 25 percent of the adult population at the time of eviction) to die between the date of eviction and the end of 1978. The immediate cause of his death was pneumonia, but he is said to have sickened shortly after he made a brief return visit in December to his old homestead.

Supported almost entirely by meager tribal resources, the majority of the fifteen families were still temporary residents in Window Rock over twelve months later. During the latter part of that period, ten of the families were evaluated by the Family Service Agency of Fort Defiance on a BIA contract. In the agency's final report (1974), the acting director wrote that the families had a marked tendency to blame officials "for each and every problem which confronts them. As a result, they have limited interest in, or ability to deal with problems in an effective manner. They have little insight into how their actions and manner can cause problems for them." Such reactions are not peculiar to these families; they are characteristic of the "dependency syndrome" that characterizes the more extreme types of forced relocation the world over. Although some of the families had drinking problems before eviction (which may or may not have been exacerbated during the lengthy period of litigation in which they were involved), alcohol abuse grew worse at Window Rock as the people continued to exist in depressing and demoralizing circumstances. Their livestock, initially corralled and fed at the fair grounds, lost condition while confined during the winter. Some died and, since the relocatees had no access to grazing land, the rest were sold. It is hardly surprising, then, that alcohol consumption increased, as did family disorganization and disputes with the hosts, who came to view the relocatees as undesirable neighbors. They became increasingly concerned about their presence in the area, which only increased relocatee insecurity and stress.

This situation has not yet improved substantially since most families have still to receive any major compensation in the form of housing and other benefits. This is contrary to the expectation of the Court of Appeals, which reaffirmed their eviction in February 1972 and stated that "there is nothing in the record to suggest that the United States will not fulfill its fiduciary obligations to appellants when this litigation is concluded" (*United States* v. *Kabinto,* 456 F. 2d 1087, 9th Circuit 1972). In fact, the United States government has so far done very little for these people.

In 1976 and 1977 Betty Beetso Gilbert Tippeconnie collected information on all fifteen families while writing her master's thesis at Arizona State University, Tempe, on District 6 relocation (Gilbert 1977). Although all the families had by then left Window Rock, dispersing to at least four chapters (all of which included some former JUA land), only one (or possibly two) was known to have a home of its own built with relocation benefits. Of the thirteen married couples living in District 6 at the time of the eviction (the other two families were headed by a widow and a widower), at least six and possibly seven had been separated either by death or divorce.

In 1978 we interviewed two of the families. One had yet to receive any relocation benefits; the other was the family known to have improved housing in 1976. Still scarred by their experiences, both reported nothing good about relocation. One husband declared, "Unhappiness is all I know." The other husband was much more explicit, reporting that:

> we felt very bad about relocation. It's really bad. We lost my father, mother, and sister [all dead since 1972] and my daughter too. They worried and [their] mind [went] kind of bad. They wandered off someplace with no place to stay. My daughter too [twenty-three years old, she was struck and killed by a car]. My wife's sister died in Gallup [she was also struck and killed by a car], and her sister's son died in Holbrook [he was killed in a fight]. Even if we have a home here we're still

having a hard time. We have to pay to haul water and wood. When we lived in Echo Canyon, we had a wagon and wagon team. And we had sheep [the family had none at their new home].

This family is convinced that all of the deaths mentioned were precipitated by the eviction.

Black Mesa Relocation. Compulsory relocation induced by coal mining on Black Mesa is also unsatisfactory in regard to benefits as well as to other special features. Fortunately, to date fewer than ten families have had to relocate, so perhaps the situation can be improved for the remaining families. One feature that makes relocation especially difficult is that land immediately to the south of the coal lease areas falls on the Hopi side of the partition line—some families are caught between strip-mining activities on the one hand and the former JUA controversy on the other. To the north of the claim area the terrain drops off precipitously to the low-lying portions of Kayenta, Shonto, and Forest Lake Chapters, which lie outside the lease areas. These chapters are unwilling to approve home-site leases for relocatees from Black Mesa. Aside from the usual hesitancy of hosts to give scarce land to relocatees, they fear that if they set a precedent for a few Black Mesa relocatees they may also be required to absorb former JUA relocatees.

As far as benefits go, Black Mesa relocatees who have legitimate claims to a customary use area are paid off at the rate of $50 per acre. An investigator from the tribe's Department of Land Administration is responsible for mapping use areas, a most difficult task since boundaries tend to overlap. Where conflicts and disagreements exist, they are brought before the tribe's Black Mesa Review Board, which adjudicates the claims and decides how the money is to be divided up. Although substantial sums may be involved, the experience with relocation the world over is that poorly educated, low-income relocatees rarely have the experience to manage large sums of cash, especially when they are far larger than any lump payment they had ever received in the past. As a result, they are apt to consider such payments as a windfall to be spent for consumer goods rather than as capital that must be carefully invested to provide a substitute living.

There is no reason to expect Navajos to behave any differently, especially since they cannot reinvest in livestock and since most are a long distance from banks and savings and loan associations. Although we do not know how Black Mesa relocatees have spent their cash benefits, we do know that those received by NIIP relocatees tend to be invested in pickup trucks and other goods with a limited life span. Indeed, one reason Burnham residents are resisting removal in connection with strip-mining is that they have observed that NIIP relocatees tend to spend their entire cash benefit within a twelve-month period, after which some are destitute.

Some relocated Black Mesa men benefit from new jobs, but this is not the case for elderly relocatees and women, who are the most seriously affected by relocation. Replacement housing is not provided, nor apparently are moving expenses or moving assistance (although we have not been able to confirm this story, one elderly relocatee, a woman, is reputed to have died of a heart attack while or after moving her few belongings). Instead, people received only the appraised value for their homes, which in the case of an old hogan is several hundred dollars at most. Such an amount is totally inadequate for building replacement housing.

Because of winter road conditions, it was not possible for members of our team to interview more than three Black Mesa relocatees. Scanty information was also collected on four others. Of the four, two began to build new houses off the lease area but ran out of money before they completed their still unlivable homes. Two others have yet to leave the lease area (although their two-year grace period is up) and so presumably are subjected to serious hazards in the form of dust, smoke from burning coal, and moving vehicles.

Two of the relocatee families that were interviewed were middle-aged couples (the third was the daughter of one of these); both husbands were among those fortunate enough to have well-paying jobs at the Peabody Mine (they made over $1,200 per

73

month). This obviously is a major benefit, and the men may well be able to transfer their skills to other jobs when the mining is finished. On the other hand, both families felt that a paid job was no substitute for one's own customary use area. Living in hogans with no electricity or piped water, both families also wanted improved housing, although this was definitely secondary to land and livestock.

The older family of the two had relocated in 1977, moving some forty miles from Forest Lake Chapter to Shonto, where they had built two small hogans in the customary use area of the wife's relatives. Since they were not allowed to transfer their livestock, they had sold all their sheep and cattle prior to moving. The move itself was caused by both the Navajo-Hopi land dispute and the Black Mesa coal leases, although it is not clear from the interview whether or not the family actually lived inside the lease areas. They had moved on their own initiative and had yet to receive any benefits either from the Navajo tribe, Peabody, or the Relocation Commission (to which they had recently applied).

The circumstances under which the interview was carried out are of significance to this report. The interviewer (Kenneth Begishe) stopped by the hogan in the morning and arranged an evening interview. When he returned that night he was told that the husband had left in anger after being told that someone was coming to interview him about removal. His wife and daughter explained that he was very upset by the relocation and had been behaving in a strange and indescribable way since the removal had taken place. He easily became angry and then left the house, although he always returned some hours later. Since they doubted that he would be willing to answer questions about relocation, Begishe began interviewing the wife instead. In the middle of the interview, the husband returned, received an explanation of the purpose of Begishe's visit, and thereafter listened quietly as his wife continued answering questions. Before the interview ended, his wife asked if he had any comments. At that point he replied, "Yes, I do have some things to say about what it is like [being a traditional Navajo] to experience the distressing effect of relocation." He then completed the remainder of the interview questions and went on to give Begishe a lengthy statement, in the middle of which he began to sob. Eventually, his sobbing made it impossible for him to continue. The following edited comments are taken from his statement:

I was born at Big Mountain at a place called Owl Springs. My mother's maternal grandfather was born there. [When] some Navajos were taken to Fort Sumner, this great-grandfather stayed behind and did not go and was still there when the people came back. This is what my mother told me and then she showed me where my great-grandfather's and great-grandmother's burial sites are. These are my reasons why I know that this land is my very own. For this land was inherited through my maternal grandmothers. Thus this land is my very own and I consider it part of my own flesh. I married my wife from Shonto [and] I took my wife back on top of Black Mesa. With much effort on my part, I built houses and I built the corral for the sheep and I built up a sizable stock of cattle and also a stock of horses. This was the way I put my life in place. And I bought a grazing permit. I also had a brand of my own. The life that I led there was a great pleasure and satisfaction to me, and I was very happy and my brain was happy, and my heart was happy, and I was very encouraged as I lived my life. I also spoke to my children about this life. "I have given birth to you all at this very place, and this is your very own land; this is your roots and you will live and multiply here throughout your life," I told them. Afterward a boundary line was made and the judge's decision of approval was made. And I heard with my own ear that my land was given to the Hopis. As a result of this I became very depressed and I grieved and cried [at this point the interviewee began to sob, continuing off and on until he could speak no further]. I cried continually for some time. Afterward as my thought settled and as my body relaxed, I was able to talk with my wife about it. "Now you will plan for us all," I told my wife. Accordingly, she returned to the place where she was born to ask for land. At this present time I am still very full of grief and it causes me to walk with grief at this time of the night. And it causes me to speak very abruptly and causes me to be sick continuously as I live on. All my sense of ownership and my sense of relating myself to this world is [now gone]. Here I am just a guest in another land. I am no longer respected at the present time. Thus I am grieving

75

continuously. The way I am crying now [the interviewee was sobbing again] is the way I continuously grieve as I live from day to day.

Earlier, during her interview, the wife had also referred to her own depression about the family's predicament. She also said that her husband's mother, who still lives on top of Black Mesa, "is very depressed and gets sick very often. Tonight she is having another ceremony [a certain medicine man is singing over her]. Ever since the land dispute she [has] had anywhere from seven to ten medicine men."

While the interview with the second family is not quite so grim, it does not make for pleasant reading. In 1972, when strip-mining began, the family moved only a short distance, apparently staying within the same customary use area. Now, however, they have been told that they must move again, and there has already been drilling around their home. In this case, the family did receive some cash benefits: the payment for their old home and outbuildings amounted to less than $1,000. In 1978, they also finally received nearly $8,000 for the disruption of their grazing area.

In discussing the negative aspects of relocation, the interviewee mentioned that "the smoke from burning coal is unbearable, especially in the morning. Everybody would be coughing, and sometimes we would get sick from it." In addition to the smoke, the interviewee and his family were troubled by dust during the drier months, and they were fearful of the heavy truck traffic. Indeed, the respondent referred to one relative whose daughter and grandson were said to have been killed when a large tire fell from a Peabody truck and struck them.

Because he was still living in part of his customary use area, this interviewee still had sheep, although he anticipated that he would have to get rid of them after his next move, since he would have no land left. Already some have been killed by vehicles and others have, in his opinion, been poisoned by waste material from the mine.

Navajo Indian Irrigation Project Relocation. As in the Black Mesa case, initial contact with NIIP relocatees is made by the tribe's Department of Land Administration, which inventories the relocatees and surveys their land and other resources. This information is then handed over to the Farmington office of the BIA, which apparently coordinates and executes the relocation program with assistance from the Indian Health Service and the tribe's CETA program.

Relocation benefits differ from those given to qualifying former JUA relocatees and to Black Mesa relocatees. In the NIIP case, benefits include purchase of the relocatee's grazing permit (if there was one) at $300 per sheep unit and the provision of decent, safe, and sanitary replacement housing, which is usually constructed by CETA trainees. While the cash benefits sometimes went as high as $30,000, the majority of the relocatees soon spent their settlement money, leaving them worse off than before. As for their new housing, all five relocatees interviewed had very negative reactions. All complained that the housing was too cold: the houses were provided with poorly designed fireplaces that did not draw properly. As a result, the relocatees had to replace them at their own expense with potbellied stoves, the flues of which were stuck through windows. They also all complained that their houses were too small for their families, and most complained that the houses were poorly built. In three cases, plumbing problems were mentioned, and in one of those the toilet had been out of commission for five months. Although the houses were electrified, those that team members inspected were certainly of a lower standard than those obtained by former JUA relocatees.

The relocatees' main complaint had to do with unfulfilled promises, especially in regard to irrigated land. At least some interviewees insisted that tribal officials had promised them land (the figure varied between five and ten acres) either in the project area or within the adjacent San Juan Valley, where apparently some uninterviewed relocatees were resettled, though on smaller irrigated holdings. They also claimed that they had been promised jobs on the project that were not forthcoming, and that they had been promised that only local people would be employed rather than other Navajos, Spanish-speakers, and Anglos.

While the promises claimed may have been exaggerated by the relocatees, it is a common practice for relocation officials the world over to "promise the moon" in order to get recalcitrant relocatees to move out. For example, the information to be discussed in Chapter 9 suggests that certain officials of the Navajo and Hopi Indian Relocation Commission initially gave chapter officials and members of planning committees the erroneous impression that chapter land was to be withdrawn for both relocatee and host housing alike, and that money was available for community facilities if the land was withdrawn. It is also apparent that tribal officials made unrealistic promises to NIIP relocatees. The five NIIP interviewees all found themselves on one-acre plots of unirrigable land close to the edge of a mesa overlooking the San Juan Valley and close to ancient Anasazi burial sites. They believed, quite justifiably it would appear, that they had been misled.

These comments do not apply only to the five interviewed relocatees, since Navajo Community College (NCC) inter-viewers at the Shiprock Campus (identified in Appendix 1) have interviewed adult members of up to thirty-eight relocated households (according to present plans at least ninety families eventually will be moved). Apparently, none of these have received irrigated land from the tribe, and some have yet to receive the utilities they were promised. At least two families were inadvertently left out of relocation planning entirely and have still to get new housing. Although we were told that relocatees removed from one section of NIIP had received irrigated land, and though a promise has been made to give relocatees from other (but not all) sections irrigated land on the project, any policy that arbitrarily gives certain benefits to some relocatees and withholds them from others is a poor one. As for cash benefits, those with few livestock got little money, even though in some cases their stock numbers were apparently low because of hardship due to a previous relocation from land being

strip-mined by Utah International. According to the NCC interviewers, even those who received substantial sums soon spent
the cash. Now without sheep or with less than ten, they were
forced to buy mutton from other Navajos or from butchers, a
situation that potential mine relocatees immediately south in
Burnham Chapter had noticed with grim foreboding.

In summarizing the data from their interviews, the NCC team
presented Thayer Scudder with the following composite reaction
of those interviewed: "We don't like relocation." Why? (1) No
more land: "Land has been passed from generation to generation." "I have no land to give to my children." "[It] seems like the
end for me." "I can't plan ahead for my children." (2) No grazing
permit, no sheep: "[There is] no income." "Nothing to keep my
kids busy." "It hurts traditionally; [there are] no sheep contribu-
tions for ceremonies." (3) The sudden change causes emotional
letdowns: "[I] can't think straight." "[I] can't think ahead for my
children." (4) Relocation causes families to fall apart: "Kids have
nothing to do." "Kids run off." "There are altercations between
family members."

The relocatees worried about the drinking of their husbands or
wives, children, and neighbors. They worried about where to get
money for their children's clothes, for food, for bills, and for
home maintenance. In the latter case, they worried about money
for painting the soot-covered walls and ceilings and for fixing
water faucets, cracked walls, leaky pipes, and poorly constructed
chimneys. Psychologically, they worried about their housing
being near Anasazi ruins ("traditionally Navajos were not
supposed to live near ruins: it's a taboo") and near strange burial
sites. They also worried about being placed on their current sites
without any choice. And they wondered, "Why did I sell out?"

SUMMARY

Although only fourteen of our interviews were carried
out among rural relocatees, we have analyzed these in some
detail because, unlike the urban relocatees, those involved are
similar to the much larger number of potential relocatees still to

79

be moved. Like the rural relocatees, the population of potential relocatees includes significant numbers of uneducated men and women over the age of forty with very strong ties to their land and livestock. Also, like so many of the rural relocatees, most of these older people can be expected to be "poor copers." Whether relocated in town or on small plots on the reservation, they will grieve for their customary use areas and for their livestock. They will also see themselves as unwilling guests on someone else's land, and they will fear that their landless children will not only scatter but lose their Navajo identity. New housing will not solve these problems. Should relocation continue as required by Public Law 93–531, at the very least Congress should ensure that sufficient replacement land is purchased to allow those who wish to do so to continue a ranching style of life. Philip Reno and his colleagues at the Shiprock, New Mexico, campus of Navajo Community College have already stressed the importance of this for the Burnham Navajos should they have to relocate. One of the Black Mesa relocatees made the same point, while all five NIIP relocatees stated that their first preference in terms of a range of options presented them was irrigated land on the irrigation project. The Black Mesa relocatee also noted that if he had to move again (as he must do), he would like the authorities to give him some land that he likes. He would also like land set aside for his children and he would like his future homesite cleared and leveled, with an improved house built there with electricity, piped water, and plumbing. These are hardly unreasonable requests for people who are being forced to give up so much.

The analysis of the rural relocatee interviews points up the very real need for relocation benefits to be standardized for all Navajos who must move, regardless of reason, and for relocation to be planned and/or coordinated by a single agency within the Navajo tribal administration. Because of prior experience and because present staff are already familiar with the problems caused by compulsory relocation, the Navajo-Hopi Land Dispute Commission is the logical agency to take over this broader responsibility.

Potential Relocatees

All Navajos who still live on the Hopi side of the partition line are potential relocatees. Thirty-six potential relocatees from eight of the eleven chapters that have lost some land to the Hopis were interviewed. Of these, 53 percent were women. The average age of the interviewees was fifty, versus forty-five for rural relocatees and thirty-seven for urban relocatees. Educational levels were low, with 49 percent having no education at all, 54 percent having four years of schooling or less, and 71 percent having eight years or less (17 percent had some high school education and 12 percent some higher education). These levels were, however, higher than for former household heads covered by the 1979 Wood, Vannette, and Andrews study. At the time of the interviews, 58 percent were unemployed, 9 percent were in CETA and other training programs, and 33 percent were employed.

Sixty-nine percent of the interviewees were currently married, while 11 percent were separated or divorced, 14 percent were widowed, and 6 percent were single (since two interviewees were children of the head of household). Seventy-eight percent of the interviewees were household heads, 17 percent spouses of heads, and 5 percent other blood relatives of household heads. The number of household members averaged 8.28; the number of household members living at home averaged 5.06.

Only three (9 percent) of the potential relocatees had positive feelings about relocation, while at least 62 percent were very concerned about moving. Fully 90 percent said that their navel cords had been buried within their customary use areas and that their minds were closely associated with that spot. Seventy-two percent had at some time promised elders, many now dead, that they would not leave their land. As potential relocatees, they were now concerned about the implications of breaking that promise. As for leaving ancestral burial grounds, 32 percent did not even wish to discuss such a sensitive topic. Of the remainder, 84 percent expressed concern about leaving the burial sites of their ancestors. More traditional than those former JUA people who have already relocated, 89 percent participated in Navajo ceremonies and/or the affairs of the Native American Church (versus 57 percent of the relocatees). They also tended to be isolated from people off the reservation; 53 percent had no children living or working in town.

As for current activities aside from wage labor, weaving was practiced in at least 58 percent of the households and silversmithing in 11 percent. Weaving requires access to sheep: 76 percent of the households still owned sheep; another 21 percent had previously owned sheep and now had none, primarily because of stock reduction. Eighty-nine percent also grew some crops on their land. Following relocation, the large majority would have to give up both their livestock and their farms, and they were aware of and seriously concerned about that threat.

Politically, potential relocatees were more active in chapter and tribal affairs and less active in state affairs than relocatees. For example, 94 percent voted in the last chapter election and 83 percent in the last tribal election, versus 70 percent and 73 percent, respectively, among all relocatees. Only 25 percent were registered for state voting, versus 42 percent of all relocatees. In spite of this more active involvement in local and tribal affairs, relationships with the tribal government were strained because of the land dispute. Many potential relocatees believed that the tribe was not active enough in attempting to repeal or amend Public Law 93–531. When asked about their relationships with the tribal administration, one-third said that they had no such relationship. As for those that did, 59 percent did not find the tribal administration helpful. Indeed, only 18 percent reported a helpful relationship. The remainder of the interviewees had a more ambiguous view of the matter.

Strained relationships between relocatees and their own government characterize all programs of compulsory relocation, since relocatees automatically interpret their removal to mean that their own elected representatives and their own government are either powerless to protect their interests or are not willing to do so. Either way, the local government loses credibility—a most unfortunate development, since it makes it harder for relocatees to work constructively with local agencies following removal. At best, relocatees simply become dependent on such agencies, and at worst (as in the District 6 case) they become suspicious or actively hostile. In the Navajo case, any undermining of the credibility of the Navajo administration also goes against the congressional intent expressed in the Indian Self-Determination Act.

With a high unemployment rate (58 percent for interviewees and 79 percent for spouses of interviewees), potential relocatees have been hard hit by the long land dispute in other ways. Ninety-one percent stated that the freeze had prevented the construction of new housing, causing either overcrowding or the scattering of children as they matured and married. Livestock reduction also increased their problems: 69 percent attributed their current financial difficulties primarily to destocking.

Seventy-two percent of the potential relocatees also worried about the impact of removal on their own children. Of those involved, 87 percent felt that the threat of relocation had already caused minor changes in their children's behavior; the other 13 percent believed that major changes had occurred. We do not know whether these concerns reflect actual changes in the behavior of children or just the belief of parents under stress that such changes have occurred. There is certainly no doubt that many potential relocatees are themselves very insecure and hence may well project their insecurities into their children. A dramatic case in point is that of a thirty-eight-year-old woman who blamed the death of her latest child on the relocation issue: "I feel that if we leave this land that we will die because we lost our home, our land that has been ours a lifetime. We worry about it when our children talk about these problems—what's going to happen to them? My latest child died recently, and I feel that somehow our child might not have wanted to live in this type of land dispute. . . . Maybe this is why she died—because it is better. I think about this all the time. I think about how life is without livestock. I cannot imagine how it would be." Throughout this interview, several children, ranging in age from three to twenty-two, were in the room. When this mother broke down and wept openly, they were obviously concerned. Indeed, it is inconceivable that children are not influenced by the extreme tension under which their parents are living.

Forty-four percent of the potential relocatees plan to stay on in their customary use areas despite the court decision that they must move. Another 6 percent try to avoid the issue by not even thinking about, let alone planning for, relocation. Of the 50 percent who are planning to move, all stated a preference to relocate on the reservation rather than move to town or to another off-reservation location.

Like the entire population of household heads and their spouses still resident on the Hopi side of the partition line, the potential relocatees are a high-risk population in terms of compulsory relocation since they score low on three of the four criteria associated with an increased capacity to cope with removal (male sex, youth, a high school education or higher, and employment). For this reason, we predict that the large majority will find relocation extremely stressful and will be overburdened with the type of problems that have already arisen among the rural relocatees. Increased rates of mental and physical illness, and perhaps increased death rates, can be expected. Whether on or off the reservation, high and medium density housing cannot be expected to play a major role in lessening the negative effects of relocation. On the contrary, because the Navajos are used to very low density housing, such an arrangement can be expected to increase the stress load by causing suspicions and conflicts among neighbors and other community members. This expected effect is discussed in more detail in Chapter 9, in which we consider the implications of the Relocation Commission's planned housing estates on chapter land. For older relocatees, the only assured way to reduce the very negative effects of removal is to acquire sufficient lands under the auspices of Public Law 93–531 to allow those who wish to do so to continue a ranching style of life.

Above: May 11, 1981: Former JUA protestors attempting to meet with BIA officials are met instead by barbed wire and an army of BIA law enforcement officers. (Photo by Lee Cannon)

Right: A relocatee sheds tears of frustration and anger over the loss of her land, her home, her livelihood. (Photo by Kenji Kawano)

Discouraged and weary residents of the former JUA gather at Red Lake Chapter House to obtain information on the partitioning. (Photo by Kenji Kawano)

Katherine Smith of Big Mountain, shown grabbing the arm of Pat Ragsdale, assistant area director of the BIA, outside the Jeddito Chapter House, where BIA and tribal officials were meeting to discuss the impoundment of livestock that took place on the preceding day (April 21, 1981). Smith asked Ragsdale to explain to the gathering why he persisted in the impoundment. Seconds later, after he refused to reply, Ragsdale was slapped in the face by another Navajo woman. (Photo by Kenji Kawano)

Protestors in Phoenix on May 19, 1981, show their resistance to the impounding of livestock. (Photo by Lee Cannon)

Demonstration in Phoenix on May 19, 1981. (Photos by Lee Cannon)

Pauline Whitesinger, potential relocatee, in the doorway of her home on the Hopi side of the partition line. (Photo by John Running)

A typical Navajo hogan *(foreground)*, with the beginnings of a new home *(background)*, on the Hopi side of the partition line. In 1972 the U.S. District Court for Arizona put a freeze on construction in the former JUA. (Photo by John Running)

Halted construction on the Hopi side of the partition line. (Photo by John Running)

Below and on the following pages: Some of the people of Big Mountain, Arizona, who face compulsory relocation. (Photos by John Running)

Joe Benally

Slim Biakaddy

Mae Shey

Ashikie Bitsie

CHAPTER 6

Conflict and Stress in Relocatee-Host Relationships

The Structure of Relocatee-Host Relationships

Compulsory relocation of rural communities almost invariably creates stress between relocatees and those among whom they are resettled, even when the relocatees and hosts are of the same ethnic group and are related through ties of kinship and marriage. Scudder has repeatedly found this situation true in connection with relocation in Africa and the Middle East. The hostile reaction of the hosts can be predicted wherever land pressure is severe, where jobs and other economic opportunities are scarce, where community services are limited, and where benefits given to the relocatees are not available to the hosts. The latter see the relocatees as increasing the pressure on a land base that is already insufficient to meet the needs of the hosts and their children. They see the relocatees competing for jobs and other scarce economic opportunities and overloading existing community services. And, largely unaware of the stress that the relocatees are undergoing, they see them favored more often than not by compensation payments and housing benefits that are unavailable to the hosts, even though the hosts are making sacrifices to accommodate the relocatees.

We predict that the relocatee-host conflict will be especially serious both in the former JUA case and everywhere else within the Navajo Reservation where compulsory relocation is required. When forced to move, relocatees throughout the world wish to remain as close to their lost homes as possible. This is understandable since it tends to keep them in a familiar habitat among familiar neighbors. As for the Navajos, we would expect most relocatees from the former JUA to desire relocation wherever possible within the boundaries of the same chapter. Parts of eleven chapters are on the Hopi side of the partition line. Aside from Hard Rock and Coal Mine Mesa, all of these also include part of the Navajo side as well as adjacent areas outside the former JUA. Hard Rock lies entirely within the former JUA, while the former JUA portion of Coal Mine Mesa lies entirely on the Hopi side of the partition line.

Relocation presents a particularly serious problem for Coal Mine Mesa residents, since adjacent areas, including the chapter headquarters, lie in the area that the Hopi also claim in connection with the Moencopi dispute. But all relocation within chapters can be expected to cause serious conflict between relocatees and hosts. Areas on the Navajo side of the partition line are currently undergoing destocking, which will reduce stock units by approximately 90 percent before herds can be rebuilt. Like the relocatees, the potential hosts are a population under stress. According to the Wood, Vannette, and Andrews survey (1979), overall the hosts felt less well-off in 1977 than they had five years before. Furthermore, the great majority did not expect their position to improve over the next five years. As for chapter members who live just outside the boundaries of the former JUA, their land continues to be heavily overstocked. It is among such a people that relocatees would prefer to move.

Aware of this preference and increasingly concerned by the negative effects of urban relocation on former JUA Navajos, the staff of the Relocation Commission has prepared a plan to relocate most of the people to housing estates adjacent to chapter headquarters, either within the former JUA, or immediately adjacent to it. This approach, although both understandable and commendable, is totally unrealistic. One cannot expect a poverty-stricken, demoralized, and depressed host population to absorb thousands of relocatees unless removal is associated with a massive rehabilitation program for both relocatees and hosts alike. Yet, as we have seen, development assistance is not included within the provisions of P.L. 93–531.

Restrictions inhibit permanent moves from one location in the Navajo Reservation to another. The relocatee must obtain a homesite lease from the tribal headquarters. Such a lease allows the relocatee to build on a half-acre plot, but it does not include permission to run sheep or other livestock on the land. Even a homesite lease is difficult to obtain since chapter residents and officials are hesitant to allow newcomers to settle land that is already insufficient for the livestock needs of current residents and to compete for jobs that are few and far between.

Our research team learned of a number of instances in which relocatees from both the former JUA and other locales were unable to obtain homesite leases. Moved to temporary quarters in Window Rock, the 1972 District 6 relocatees were unable to obtain homesite leases within the vicinity; indeed, their relationships with the hosts became particularly strained. The few families of Black Mesa relocatees have also had difficulty in obtaining homesite leases even within the same chapter. For example, the Kayenta Chapter (headquartered in the lowlands below Black Mesa) did not wish to approve homesite applications for the few households who had to move from the top of Black Mesa. Granted this hesitancy to approve the requests of even small numbers of relocatees, the unwillingness of surrounding chapters to welcome much larger numbers of relocatees is understandable.

Even where chapters are willing to approve applications for homesite leases, the process of approval is a long one since each lease must first be approved by those currently using the land where the relocatee wishes to move. Customary use areas tend to overlap, so permission is often needed from several users. Even if the relocatee wants only to build a house, other users will be hesitant to give their approval since, once resident in the area, the relocatee may then try to acquire sheep and other stock. Even if approval is given by all involved, the application for a homesite lease must then be approved by the chapter, processed by the tribal Land Administration Department, and finally approved by the chairman of the Tribal Council and the BIA. The whole process is apt to take at least a year and in some cases may drag on indefinitely. It may be brought to a halt if members of a single household with existing rights to the customary use area involved decide to change their minds.

Navajos living on the Hopi side of the partition line are well aware of the difficulties involved in obtaining homesite leases elsewhere on the reservation. That is why a good number of them have requested off-reservation relocation. In 1978 the Relocation Commission estimated that this group made up 40 percent of the potential relocatees. The Relocation Commission reports that this number prefers off-reservation relocation, but the use of the word "prefers" is misleading. While it is true that some younger families wish to relocate off the reservation (especially those already living in town), others are requesting off-reservation housing simply because they believe they have no other alternative. Furthermore, they are fearful that if they do not move now, the supply of available housing will be exhausted, requiring them to move even farther away. A number of relocatees interviewed during our study gave this fear as one reason why they moved when they did. They were also concerned about rumors that relocation benefits (other than incentive payments) would be reduced if they delayed removal.

Although sixty-four households moved off the reservation by the end of 1978 under the Relocation Commission's Voluntary Relocation Program, it is important to understand that few of these families wanted to give up their customary use areas. Because of twenty years of neglect and uncertainty within the former JUA, and because of the difficulty of obtaining homesite leases elsewhere on the reservation, they chose urban relocation as the lesser evil. In effect, most of the urban relocatees have been forced out of the former JUA and off the reservation. Some of those in our sample now wish to return to the reservation; the majority of women and older men are worried about maintaining their Navajo identity and that of their children. All said that none of their relatives planned now to relocate off the reservation.

Similarly, none of the potential relocatees were planning an off-reservation move, suggesting that the Relocation Commission's figure of 40 percent no longer reflects the "preferences" of potential relocatees.

Analysis of Host Interviews

Twenty-four host interviews were carried out in four of the eleven chapters that include land on the Hopi side of the partition line. They included two of the four chapters in which the Relocation Commission would like to relocate forty or more families in housing estates built in the proximity of chapter headquarters. Twenty respondents were men and only four were women. Although sixteen (66.6 percent) were over forty years of age, the level of education was relatively high: fourteen (58 percent) had at least some high school education, while only seven (29 percent) had no education at all. In part, this was because one interviewer intentionally sought out English-speakers, while an effort was also made to include some Tribal Council delegates, as well as chapter and grazing committee officials.

Many of the interviewers' questions were attitudinal, i.e., respondents were asked for their opinions about different options that might be open to the relocatees. Almost invariably, respondents were sympathetic to the plight of the relocatees and distressed that the relocatees should find themselves in their present predicament, which they were more inclined to blame on the United States government than on the Hopis. When asked what would be the best plan for the relocatees, 50 percent stated that they should not move, although this answer was not one of the options they had been asked to discuss in earlier questions. Subsequently, all respondents were asked about the relocation plans of any relatives they might have on the Hopi side. Of the fifteen (62.5 percent) who had such information, seven said that their relatives did not plan to move (in two cases they volunteered the belief that they would fight rather than leave

89

voluntarily), and another five said that their relatives wanted to stay where they were currently residing.

Quite clearly, this reaction of potential relocatees was considered natural by our respondents, granted the close relationship between the Navajos and the land—especially the land on which they were born—and the belief that the land in question has always been Navajo land. Leaving the land was frequently mentioned as a major disadvantage of relocation and as a probable cause of future depression and loneliness. In the words of one fifty-one-year-old man who had been trained as a health worker, "The land is regarded as a sacred and significant part of [the] Navajo way, and tangibly the land is a strong source of pride. If these [factors] are not recognized people will become depressed and become ill." To the Navajo, "land is his mother and for all purposes our ancestors are still in the earth, and these are values and sacred to us." In evaluating options that involved moving away from one's current locale, respondents frequently gave negative evaluations simply because separation from the land was involved. When asked about the option of moving to town, for example, one eighty-two-year-old host interviewee with no education replied, "I don't know. . . . I think it will be bad. [X] moved into town. They say that they [X and his relatives, presumably] are very lonely for their land, they are in terrible shape."

When the interviewer asked about movement to land that would be bought by the tribe, a similar answer was given: "I am not sure, but I keep thinking they will still be lonely for their land. I believe many Navajos will refuse to move there even if they get the land." Yet another uneducated host responded to the same question: "No, the relocatees will still be subject to a different environment. Nothing will replace someone's birthplace and their forefathers' and mothers'. Here Navajos identify each section of the land by name in their own language."

In spite of their sympathetic attitude, when asked if they would vote for withdrawal of chapter land to house relocatees, nine hosts said "no" and seven said "yes." Another seven were indecisive. Some of them said they would vote with the majority;

others said that how they voted would depend on the exact nature of the housing estates, the implication being that if the hosts would also benefit from them (through improved housing) then their vote would be favorable. As to whether or not they would allow kin to bring stock with them should they move onto their land, eleven respondents said "no." Only five replied in the affirmative. Another five hedged their answers, saying, for example, that "we'll have to see which person asks." Four others said that the decision would not be theirs but that of the household head. As for those who said "no," their reason usually was associated with competition for limited grazing: "If I let my relatives come to my area, I know I will get a lot of resentment from neighbors"; or "No, to share grazing is an impossibility even among close relatives"; and "No, that will never be allowed, there would be too much problem of livestock reduction."

In sum, though sympathetic, the hosts felt that the potential relocatees should stay where they were. The majority were either hesitant about absorbing relatives within their own chapter or against the idea. This reaction suggests that the housing estate plan of the Relocation Commission faces opposition not just at the tribal level but also at the local level.

CHAPTER 7

Navajo Relocation, Bureaucratic Complexity, and the Challenge to Navajo Autonomy

Introduction

Part of the costs of removal for the relocatees can be attributed to their relationships with those agencies that control their lives. In the former Joint Use Area situation these include the Navajo and Hopi Indian Relocation Commission (which is responsible to the executive branch of the federal government), the Flagstaff Administrative Office of the Bureau of Indian Affairs (established in 1973 to administer the former JUA as a separate entity), the Indian Health Service, and the Navajo and Hopi Tribal Councils, not to mention various state, county, and local agencies that come to bear on former JUA Navajos when they relocate off the reservation. Even under normal circumstances the BIA, the Indian Health Service, and the Navajo tribal government determine their plans and priorities independently; no institutionalized mechanisms for coordination exist. The situation becomes even more complex when additional agencies such as the Navajo and Hopi Indian Relocation Commission and the Hopi tribal government become involved, and when the people affected are a traumatized population full of anxiety as to their future yet with virtually no influence over what that future will be.

Forced relocation, like a natural disaster, affects the whole spectrum of human life and therefore involves the many agencies already set up to deal with the range of human needs:

providing immediate assistance in finding housing, jobs, and other economic support; educating children and retraining adults; caring for the ill, the old, and the disabled who can no longer support themselves. The compulsory relocation of large numbers of people puts a major strain upon their resources. Few agencies have funding that is flexible enough to permit them to undertake a large new case load and at the same time continue to meet the needs of their regular clients. They also find it difficult to coordinate their activities in the novel fashion that an emergency situation requires. Under these circumstances, planners and policy makers usually assign part of their role, but only part, to one or more new agencies created specifically to deal with the relocation problem. Such agencies have a specific mission that tends to isolate them from existing agencies, which see them as a threat to long-established spheres of influence. They also usually have a fixed lifetime after which, task accomplished, they are expected to expire. This expectation in itself is unrealistic, given the fact that agencies, like communities, usually give priority to their own survival.

Where relocation calls for massive new funding, the appearance of a new major planning, implementing, and management agency that impinges upon local autonomy is to be expected. Those who provide the funding, typically the central administration, question the ability of existing agencies, and especially of local bodies and local personnel, to plan development and use funds efficiently. They therefore establish their own organization of both administrators and technical staff, answerable to the central government rather than to the local people. As illustrated by the history of compulsory relocation around the world, all too often the consequences are the undermining of respect for local government and its personnel, since their role is restricted and their control over those matters of most importance to the potential relocatees is in question.

Another global feature of compulsory relocation is rarely admitted. Agency staff members dealing with people who seem to have difficulties that go on and on develop what is now being called "the burnt-out syndrome." The overload on their sympathies and their ability to empathize is too great to be handled. They cope by developing an increasing personal detachment, a protective "not caring." The result, at best, is routine treatment; at worst, there is a denial of the rights of those who apply for help—who begin to inspire active dislike. The relocatees come to be held responsible for their troubles. Any questioning of staff decisions or attempts at independent action are interpreted as attacks on the wisdom of the staff.

While our charge did not include evaluating the capabilities of such organizations as the Navajo and Hopi Indian Relocation Commission, the BIA, and the Navajo tribal government to execute relocation, the general features outlined in the preceding paragraphs are all visible when one looks at the organizations involved in the relocation of Navajos from the former JUA.

Institutional Inadequacies

Existing agencies have neither the labor force, the equipment, nor the funds to meet the needs of those who are being forced to leave their land and homes. It does not matter whether the agencies called on to cope with these needs are part of the Navajo tribal administration or associated with the administrative structures of the federal, state, or local governments of border cities. Relocation is a strain on their budgets, their organization, and the human sympathies of their workers. They cannot shift resources to care for those who are being relocated without antagonizing other citizens who see no reason why normal services should diminish because other people have been forced out of their homes. While people share gracefully in a short-term emergency, relocation is a long-term situation. To date, only hundreds of people have moved; there are thousands still to come. Yet already there are signs that staff workers have begun the process of distancing themselves from the human tragedy: bewildered, angry, frightened people are being recast as demanding clients about whom funny stories can be told. By emphasizing this point, we are not criticizing individuals within the BIA and the Navajo tribal government but are indicating that the expected estrangement of administrators, tribal councilmen, and others from the relocatees has already begun to occur, as it has in all other programs of compulsory relocation.

Institutional Inconsistencies

Agency bureaucracies are responding to relocation in two mutually contradictory ways. First, they deny responsibility for those who are being relocated. The Navajo tribal agencies seek to hold the federal government or various commercial companies responsible for the consequences of land expropriation (as in the case of the former JUA) or land use (as in the case of coal and uranium mining); they expect them to cope with the needs of those who are being displaced. In some cases, the tribal agencies look to the border cities to cope with the needs of those Navajos who resettle in the towns under the Navajo and Hopi Indian Relocation Commission's program of "voluntary" relocation. However, the towns argue that the federal government, through the BIA, or the Navajo Nation must provide the support systems for the new arrivals. The federal, state, and county agencies expect the Navajo Nation to make a major effort to care for its own people, somehow absorbing them into already overcrowded chapters and finding tribal funds to buy up new land and develop new job opportunities. The question of who is to provide health care in the border towns is also a bone of contention.

Second, existing organizations have also begun to enter into an increasing rivalry for additional funding, which usually provides for vastly increased staff. The very real problems associated with relocation are therefore being exploited in the power plays that are endemic to bureaucracy. Existing agreements about who should do what are being questioned, making it more difficult for those who need help to get action.

Formation of New Institutions

Agencies newly created to cope with relocation have appeared on the scene. The Navajo and Hopi Indian Relocation Commission, created by Public Law 93–531 and responsible to the White House, is the largest of these, but the Navajo-Hopi Land Dispute Commission plays a comparable role within the Navajo Nation. The new creations are following predictable paths: they seek to widen their mission, enter into rivalries with established agencies whose functions they begin to usurp, and acquire a degree of permanence as they entrench themselves. The Navajo and Hopi Indian Relocation Commission is already facing the expected problems of isolation and noncooperation from other agencies, including the Department of the Interior, which theoretically should be a close collaborator. But bureaucracies do not behave in that manner, especially when they are competing for influence over the same population and geographical area. The Relocation Commission's Interim Progress Report (1978) amply demonstrates the difficulties the Relocation Commission is having in carrying out its duties. Indeed, it is already taking on the cast of a "pariah agency," not because of staff inadequacies but because of its very existence as an organization. As the Relocation Commission points out (1978: 27), an initially close relationship with the Office of the Secretary of the Interior "has suffered a serious setback," which the Relocation Commission regrets "even more than the serious breach of faith that this matter [the Relocation Commission's grave fiscal crisis of fiscal year 1978] represents."

As is the case with all relocation authorities, the relationship between the relocatees and the Relocation Commission is strained at best. Throughout our interviews with actual and potential relocatees, the theme of Relocation Commission misinformation and duplicity constantly reappeared. The point is not whether the Relocation Commission is acting in an appropriate fashion, but rather that most relocatees do not trust the Relocation Commission. Some even accuse it of deliberately confusing and misleading them. Complaints cover a wide range of topics. Among potential relocatees whose homes and improvements had been appraised, 44 percent complained that they had not been told the value of the appraisal. As for relocatees, they said that they were not told the value of their housing, outbuildings, and other improvements at the time of the appraisal. When they were informed of the value, it was only during the hectic days when they were actually moving and buying a new house. By then, the time had passed for lodging an appeal if the relocatees thought the appraised value was unfair, as many of them did. Respondents also thought that they had been given misinformation by certain staff members of the Relocation Commission and had been pressured into moving by being told that replacement housing might not be available for them if they did not move right away, or that subsequent relocation would be much further away from the reservation. Because of such alleged statements and because of a wide variety of rumors circulating within the former JUA (such rumors characterize all relocation programs), some elderly relocatees stated that their moves were motivated by fear.

When the Navajo and Hopi Indian Relocation Commission was first established in 1975, the three appointed commissioners, who were and still are responsible for policy, defined their task primarily as one of providing replacement housing for the relocatees. As time passed, and the commissioners and Relocation Commission staff have become more knowledgeable (as in the case of most relocation agencies, senior staff initially knew virtually nothing about relocation or those who must relocate), they have expanded their scope to include other activities. By the end of 1978, for example, the commissioners had reversed their previous position of neutrality in regard to the purchase of additional lands for the relocatees; they had become strong advocates of land acquisition. They had also come to question the wisdom of relocating Navajos household by household off the reservation. Thus, a prominent feature of the 1978 Interim Progress Report is a major plan to relocate almost 50 percent of potential relocatees in housing estates close to existing chapter headquarters. These estates would theoretically be provided with up-to-date community facilities and services. Indeed, the senior staff of the Relocation Commission has concluded that job training and economic development is also essential and should come under the mandate of the commission.

To improve its effectiveness and to improve interagency communication, coordination, and performance as they relate to relocation, the Relocation Commission would also like to increase its influence and even authority over other agencies, including the Navajo tribal government. That the Relocation Commission is seeking a new mandate is made clear in the concluding chapter of its 1978 Interim Progress Report:

> The Relocation Commission's experience suggests that there are two alternative ways to insure special delivery to relocatees. The Relocation Commission must be able to directly provide services, etc., if other agencies fail to meet relocatees' needs. Alternatively, the Relocation Commission must be able to influence the actions and programs of individual agencies which impinge on, or could contribute to, the implementation of P.L. 93-531.
>
> The first way to achieve programmatic coordination to deliver needed services involves giving the Relocation Commission the ability to engage in resettlement community development activities. The second way to achieve programmatic coordination involves giving the Relocation Commission the ability to review and comment on the programs, budgets, etc., of other federal agencies and the Navajo and Hopi tribes. Both of these strategies entail special actions—the former requires the passage of special legislation, and the latter requires designating the Relocation Commission a regional clearing house. . . . [whereby the Commission could] evaluate, review, and comment on the allocation, and the adequacy, of federal and tribal resources impinging on the implementation of P.L. 93-531. [Pp. 153-54]

The growing awareness of and concern about the negative effects of relocation on the part of the commissioners and the staff of the Relocation Commission is commendable. Their desire to increase the scope of the Relocation Commission's activities is understandable; indeed, the Relocation Commission can argue, and argue legitimately, that it cannot carry out its mission unless it can gain control over the activities and budgets of those agencies that should serve the interests of its own clients. On the other hand, major increases in Relocation Commission activities, funding, influence, and authority inevitably put in question the ability of the Navajo Nation to govern itself, just as federally funded programs in the cities have challenged city governments. In this regard, the expanding goals of the Relocation Commission are contrary to those of P.L. 93–638, the Indian Self-Determination Act. We believe P.L. 93–638 should take precedence. While we sympathize with the concerns of the Relocation Commission, in this case we believe that activities that tend to undermine the influence and authority of the Navajo tribal government are not justified.

Negative Implications for the Navajo Tribal Government

Relocation has begun to undermine the influence of the Navajo tribal government. In fact, former JUA relocation places the Navajo tribal government in an almost untenable position. To maintain credibility among the relocatees and their supporters, the tribal government has to fight relocation to the bitter end. In this regard, the unwillingness of the tribal Advisory Council to approve the withdrawal of chapter land for housing estates is predictable since such an action would amount to a tacit admission by the tribe not only that relocation was going to occur but also that the tribe was impotent to prevent it. It would also undermine the tribe's attempt, through the 1978 DeConcini Amendment to P.L. 93–531, to obtain life estates for certain categories of people, since existence of approved housing estates and community facilities around chapter headquarters would call into question the criteria on which life estates were to be based. On the other hand, should Congress proceed with P.L. 93–531, with or without amendments, the continued opposition of the tribal government is contrary to the interests of those currently living on the Hopi side of the partition line, since opposition will only prolong the stress period prior to the completion of

99

relocation. So long as relocation is required, the tribal government is in a "no win" situation; indeed, it is already suffering from popular discontent over its handling of the former JUA situation. Outside the former JUA, Navajos are becoming impatient as the conflict drags on and on, with increased expenditure of time and financial resources that they believe could be better-used elsewhere. This is characteristic of the type of hardening of attitudes among nonrelocatees that is a feature of all relocation programs. As for relocatees and potential relocatees, many have little use for the tribal government and its representatives. As the conflict continues, they can be expected to turn more and more to other organizations for assistance, as has already happened in the Big Mountain area, where some potential relocatees have sought the assistance of the Relocation Commission or the American Indian Movement (AIM). In either case, the influence of the duly elected tribal government is undermined, contrary to the intent of P.L. 93–638.

CHAPTER 8

The Excessive Financial
Costs of Relocation

In our experience with programs of compulsory relocation throughout the world, governments and relocation agencies
tend to underestimate and/or underbudget the costs of removal
by a factor of three or four. This is also the case in connection
with P.L. 93–531. While the law directed the Navajo and Hopi
Indian Relocation Commission to identify relocation sites and to
assure that both housing and community facilities would be
available to the relocatees, less than $50 million was stipulated
for carrying out the job. According to the plan outlined in the
Relocation Commission's Interim Progress Report (1978), the
current cost of providing community facilities alone is estimated
at $93,580,500. This does not include the costs of housing, and
incentive payments, as well as the recurrent expenses of the
Relocation Commission. Leaving aside the costs of livestock
reduction, range rehabilitation, fencing, and so on, which fall
more appropriately under economic development, the total costs
for relocation, housing, community facilities, and administrative
expenses can be expected to approach $150 million. But this is
according to current cost estimates and does not take cost
increases into consideration. Since it is reasonable to expect that
most of these facilities will not be constructed for several years,
the final costs for these items could easily come to $250 million.
Indeed, separate estimates by two senior staff members of the
Relocation Commission for the final costs of community facilities alone were $150 million and $200 million. These estimates
do not include the increased costs of medical and other essential
services for urban relocatees, nor do they include costs for

101

improved housing among the hosts, an expenditure that we believe to be essential if the necessary cooperation of the hosts and chapter officials is to be obtained.

In other words, once all expenses are totaled, the cost of relocation without the minimal housing program needed to obtain host support and without any economic development program can be conservatively estimated at a quarter of a billion dollars. However, allocation of that amount will not significantly improve the lot of either the relocatees or their hosts. On the contrary, it can be expected to increase welfare dependency among the former and competition over land and economic opportunities among the latter.

It is not possible to put financial costs on human suffering, let alone on disruptions that may cause mental or other illness and premature death. For this reason, economists tend to agree that it is not possible to estimate, in financial terms, the human costs of relocation. As a result, those legislating and executing programs that involve relocation tend to underestimate, or ignore altogether, the human costs just as they underestimate the numbers of people involved and the financial costs of their removal. This situation is most unfortunate since presumably legislatures and planners would consider other options more seriously if they had a more accurate understanding of both the human and financial costs of compulsory relocation.

A method pioneered by Philip Reno provides perhaps the best approach to computing the financial costs of relocation. This requires an estimate of the costs of reintegrating relocatees in a useful role in Navajo society without making others worse off in the process. Though this approach does not compensate for stress during the transition period, it does try to bring the transition period to a close at the earliest possible moment through a process of rehabilitation and reintegration. At the very least, rehabilitation and reintegration should ensure that the relocatees and hosts are no worse off once the transition period is over than they were prior to relocation. Public Law 93–531 does not meet this standard, let alone provide for funds in such a way that their cost effectiveness is improved by directly raising both the productivity and the standards of living of the relocatees. We use the word "directly" intentionally, since improved access to such community facilities as schools will improve the employability of the younger generation of Navajos. In that sense, the preliminary plan of the Relocation Commission will indirectly benefit Navajo youth—but it will not increase the productivity of those past school age.

Reno and his colleagues at the Navajo Community College (NCC), Shiprock, New Mexico, have been involved in a study (funded by the Environmental Protection Agency) of the advantages and disadvantages of strip-mining in the Burnham area. One of the major disadvantages is that an unknown number of people will be required to move if mining occurs. These people are already familiar with many of the problems that accompany relocation since they are aware of the negative effects of compulsory relocation on those removed from the land set aside for the Navajo Indian Irrigation Project. In assessing this situation, the NCC study team has tried to ascertain the type of compensation the people would prefer if relocation is required. Their requests strike us as very reasonable. What they want is:

> to move together, by and large, to a new area where they can recreate in some meaningful way the lives they must give up. They do not hope for restoration of their life in its entirety. They do ask land enough, however, to afford some privacy, at least a few sheep, maintenance of a working nucleus of their kinfolk and neighbors, and through all this, a chance for a useful role in Navajo society. The demands represent community consensus, not the usual individual calculus that can be so easily broken down in bargaining.
>
> Meeting the community's wishes or demands requires a well-worked-out relocation program—providing land, training, education and job opportunities, social services and housing. [Reno 1978: 5]

These components are equally necessary for the large majority of potential former JUA relocatees. Although the senior staff within the Relocation Commission is now thinking along these lines, P.L. 93–531 contains funds only for the housing component. As we have argued throughout, this is totally inadequate. If compulsory relocation is in fact going to be carried out according to congressional intent, additional land must be acquired for those who wish to continue a ranching style of life, and funds must be made available not just for housing but also for social services and economic development. Furthermore, in the former JUA case these efforts need to be directed toward both relocatees and hosts alike. The financial costs of such an exercise can be expected to approach half a billion dollars. Given the present state of the economy, and the increasing pressures on Congress and the executive branch to end deficit spending, it is exceedingly unlikely that even a significant fraction of this sum will be allocated.

CHAPTER 9

Options for Future Congressional Action

Introduction

We believe that Congress should assess carefully the advantages and disadvantages of three major options: carrying out P.L. 93–531 as currently written; amending P.L. 93–531; and repealing P.L. 93–531. Of the three options, we believe that repeal is the most advantageous, provided it is linked with a land purchase and development program for the Hopis. We also believe that carrying out P.L. 93–531 as currently written is the most disadvantageous. At the time of its enactment, the number of people to be relocated, the human costs of relocation, and the financial costs of relocation were all seriously underestimated. If P.L. 93–531 is to be carried out according to congressional intent, a much larger sum of money than originally planned and a number of amendments to the law will be necessary. Otherwise, the relocation program will prove extremely stressful not just for the majority of the relocatees but also for the hosts and the Navajo tribal administration.

Priority Number One: Former Joint Use Area Development

Whatever option is selected, the former JUA desperately needs development to make up for decades of government-induced neglect. This should be integrated rural and urban-industrial development that involves major economic, social

105

service, and housing components. Ideally, it requires integrated planning for the entire Navajo Reservation, the Hopi Reservation (however it comes to be defined), and the border regions. While this may not be possible for political reasons, it does not make sense to design separate and relatively uncoordinated development plans for the Hopi Reservation, for the Navajo portion of the former JUA, for the relocatees, and for the rest of the Navajo Reservation.

Where Navajos are involved, the Navajo tribal government should play a major role. Currently the tribal government is building up a planning capacity within its Division of Economic Development. This capacity should be encouraged and supported by Congress since it is a basic requirement if the goals of P.L. 93–638 (the Indian Self-Determination Act) are to be realized. At the same time, Congress should spell out mechanisms to ensure consultation, coordination, and a division of labor between the Navajo government and the various federal agencies, including the BIA, the Indian Health Service, and, in the event that relocation continues, the Relocation Commission.

According to P.L. 93–531, the Relocation Commission should develop its plan "to the maximum extent feasible in consultation with the persons involved in such relocation and appropriate representatives of their tribal councils." In fact, very little involvement is occurring. This is not the fault of the staff within the Relocation Commission or within the tribal government. Forced community relocation the world over is characterized by lack of relocatee participation. Since relocatees do not want to move, they resist involvement in the planning process. Taking their cue from their constituents, the staff and representatives of the local government also resist involvement in the planning process, since relocation threatens their own legitimacy. The result is an adversary relationship that is hardly conducive to planning. Even if this can be kept under control, it is not easy (indeed, perhaps a contradiction in terms) for a powerful and highly centralized Relocation Commission to share its power to plan and implement relocation and development with the relocatees and their local representatives.

For such reasons, planning capabilities should be built up within the tribal government, while major execution capabilities should be strengthened within the tribal government and also within the BIA, the Indian Health Service, and, should relocation continue, the Relocation Commission. Planning should be bold and imaginative; the serious nature of the problem requires no less. Because of a complex of historical and situational factors, including the land dispute itself and the building freeze, the former JUA is one of the most isolated and undeveloped places in the United States. To revitalize this area will require new approaches to development and major funding.

Recently the Navajo government (including various government-run agencies such as the Navajo Tribal Utility Authority), the BIA, and the Indian Health Service were involved in a major effort to assess the needs of the former JUA (Bureau of Indian Affairs 1978; Navajo Nation 1978a). Although some of this assessment includes the relocatees, the Relocation Commission did not play an active part. While useful, this needs assessment exercise should not be considered a substitute for a development plan since little effort has been made to date to integrate and give priorities to the various components. One such component put forward by the tribe's Division of Economic Development was a proposed economic impact study that "will analyze the wants and needs of the people, identify all available resources (land, labor, etc.) and assess alternative economic development options." More specifically, the impact study will have the following goals: (1) to study in depth alternative economic development options for the former JUA; (2) to identify potential economic development projects tailored to the area and its people; (3) to identify all available resources; (4) to project capital and labor requirements of identified projects; (5) to provide, as an end result, a comprehensive economic development plan for the former JUA, which will be used to request funding.

Though a good proposal, this impact study should be carried out within the context of the wider area and, if relocation continues, consider the relocatees as well as those now living on the Navajo side of the partition line. This means that careful

coordination would be necessary between the tribe's Division of
Economic Development, the Navajo-Hopi Land Dispute Commission, and the Relocation Commission.

The impact study is linked to a general request for planning
assistance. Out of the budget for this assistance, $125,000 would
be earmarked for the impact study. While this may be sub-
contracted, it will constantly be "subject to the scrutiny and
control of the Navajo planning personnel of the former JUA." An
additional $457,966 is requested for planning assistance over a
five-year period, starting at $79,637 for Year One and building
up to $104,386 for Year Five. The project itself is divided into
three phases. The planning staff will be hired during the first
phase, "and the impact study will be initiated and completed."
This is allotted nine months. During the next three months of
the first year (the second phase), "comprehensive planning for
the economic development projects will begin." The third phase,
which will last four years, will be concerned with the implementation of the plan with respect to specific projects.

Such an effort in comprehensive planning by the tribe is a
necessary first step. It should precede the implementation of a
wide range of specific projects, which all too often are conceived in
isolation from each other and the general sociocultural context of
the target area. It is absolutely essential to involve the Navajo
population in these projects at the chapter level. "Involve" here
has two meanings. The first is to actively involve the people in
the design, implementation, management, and evaluation of
development efforts. After all, they will be the main beneficiaries
if the development is relatively successful—and the main victims
if it is relatively unsuccessful. As the principal risk takers, they
should participate in the development process. Second, development should be designed in such a way that it involves the Navajo
sociocultural system itself. In other words, it should be a
development program adapted to Navajo conditions, one that
builds on local strengths and offsets local weaknesses.

Although working closely with the BIA, the Indian Health
Service, and the Relocation Commission, the responsible organizations in this development program would be the Navajo tribe's

Division of Economic Development and the Navajo-Hopi Land Dispute Commission. The materials presented in the two needs assessment volumes provide important background material for this project. Three major priorities emerge from these two documents, which represent the efforts of separate departments and agencies: the first is a major road construction and maintenance program; the second is a major educational program; and the third is the planning of a growth center at Piñon that would include a major educational complex (kindergarten through high school plus vocational training and adult education) and a new district center for law enforcement and judicial services.

These priorities appear to be sound, but they need to be carefully thought through in terms of an ongoing program of integrated rural and urban-industrial development for the Navajo Reservation as a whole. While physical and social infrastructure are crucial, as are a wide range of governmental and nongovernmental services, the two needs assessment volumes are weak on the generation of employment opportunities in connection with agriculture (here defined to include crop production, livestock management, and forestry), small-scale businesses and cottage industries, tourism, mining, labor-intensive industry, and so on. For example, one section in the needs assessment reports deals with the need for a revolving fund to provide credit for small Navajo-run businesses. This certainly is an important component. On the other hand, the reports contain no information on what sort of small businesses and cottage industries should be encouraged. As for labor-intensive industry, we talked to a number of senior staff members both within and without the Navajo government about their ideas for a range of factories that would produce such items as clothing, cinder blocks, and plastic and electronic components, but no one had worked through such ideas in the context of an overall development plan. That is why the planning proposal of the Navajo Division of Economic Development should be funded and implemented at the earliest possible moment.

It is important for Congress to understand that the financial cost of a major development program for the former JUA will be

109

high. The costs of the more expensive draft proposals included within the two 1978 needs assessment volumes (Bureau of Indian Affairs 1978; Navajo Nation 1978a), although they are not integrated and do not deal directly with the provision of employment opportunities, total over $400 million. This does not include the cost of former JUA relocation, which can conservatively be estimated at $200 million if relocation is carried out according to congressional intent in regard to replacement housing and supporting community services. And this does not include the costs for Hopi development. Clearly, the rehabilitation of the former JUA is going to be a costly operation. This is why we emphasize the need for very careful integrated planning that pays close attention to the local sociocultural environment as well as that of the Arizona-New Mexico region. We believe that Congress should endorse such an effort regardless of its final decision on relocation simply because the United States government is largely responsible for the present predicament of the residents of the former JUA.

Carrying Out Public Law 93–531 as Currently Written

This option has one major advantage and four major disadvantages. The advantage is to the Hopis since it gives them control of and access to one-half of the former JUA. The disadvantages are that (1) it will cause extreme multidimensional stress among a great many Navajos; (2) it will reduce the influence of the Navajo Tribal Council; (3) it will be very expensive; and (4) because of unanticipated problems, it will be more difficult to carry out relocation than was expected at the time P.L. 93–531 was passed.

MULTIDIMENSIONAL STRESS

This report has summarized the evidence that the multidimensional stress associated with other programs of compulsory relocation—regardless of the locale, the ethnic background of the relocatees, and the policy of the relocation authorities—is equally applicable to the Navajos. Indeed, we have argued that it can be expected to be more severe in the Navajo case than in many situations elsewhere because of the strong ties to land and community that characterize the Navajos, because of their poverty and (among the large majority of those over the age of forty) their illiteracy, and because of their already depressed and dependent state, owing to the long-standing land dispute.

The desire of Congress under Section 13 of P.L. 93–531 that the Relocation Commission's Report and Plan "take into account the adverse social, economic, cultural and other impacts of relocation on persons involved in such relocation and be developed to avoid or minimize, to the extent possible, such impacts" is commendable. On the other hand, this wording shows that Congress has not been well informed about the nature of compulsory relocation, especially for low-income ethnic populations with strong community ties, since by its very nature such relocation is extremely stressful. Major negative effects can be expected. They cannot be avoided. They can be minimized, but only through a total approach to relocation that includes economic development as well as community and social services and improved housing. Congress has not taken such an approach, so P.L. 93-531 as written is not designed even to minimize the adverse effects of relocation.

Compulsory relocation can be expected to cause the following types of stress, which are interrelated.

Psychophysiological Stress. The evidence clearly shows that relocation is causing psychological problems among both relocatees and potential relocatees. Already the Relocation Commission is extremely concerned over the adjustment of approximately 25 percent of the families that have moved off the reservation (1979), while Martin Topper's Indian Health Service report (1979) shows that use of mental health facilities by potential relocatees is already twice that of all Navajos on the reservation and eight times that of those living on the Navajo side of the partition line. On the basis of our eighty-four

111

interviews and our experience with relocation elsewhere we predict that the situation will get worse.

Of course, mental illness has an impact on the total health of relocatees and potential relocatees. There is already evidence that certain types of compulsory relocation are responsible for temporary increases in the death rate, especially among the elderly. This evidence comes both from studies of the relocation of the elderly from one custodial care center to another (Killian 1970) and from dam relocation. Several researchers plan to initiate studies for monitoring the health of Navajo relocatees. We predict that these studies will document an increased mortality rate among adult Navajos associated with the relocation period. Certainly Navajos believe that elderly people have already died because of the land dispute and because of actual relocation and the threat of relocation. The high adult death rate among District 6 relocatees since their removal in 1972 lends credence to this belief. Depression would appear to be a major contributing factor, leading either directly to death, in the case of the very old, or indirectly, through increased alcohol consumption followed by death through accidents, exposure, and so on. Congress should consider very carefully the evidence on this point.

Economic Stress. If P.L. 93–531 is carried out according to congressional intent in regard to both the provision of housing and community services, it will cost at least $200 million according to the plan being prepared by the Relocation Commission. This plan does not include economic development because Congress did not address itself to that issue. We predict that a major effect of relocation as legislated will be to make more Navajos more dependent on general assistance. In other words, the large financial outlay needed to implement the law will increase economic dependence (along with the stress associated with being unable to support oneself and one's family). Increased economic dependence can be forecast for two reasons: (1) Most Navajos will not be able to relocate with their stock. Accordingly, on the average, they will lose the 25 percent of their net income (prior to destocking) that comes from livestock management. In most cases, this will be a permanent loss. The Navajo side of the partition line is already fully utilized for stock. Although BIA experts believe that the hosts can rebuild their herds to pre-destocking levels if proper range restoration and management occur, there is no possibility that new herds could be allocated grazing land. (2) Relocatees' expenses in town and in new housing both on and off the reservation will be higher than they were before, even without inflation.

Sociocultural Stress. The sociocultural implications of re-moving Navajos from their land are major, since their identity as Navajos and their well-being are closely associated with the knowledge that there is always a customary use area on the reservation to which they can return, regardless of what happens to them off the reservation. For many potential re-locatees, removal will extinguish their ties to the land, since those customary use areas in which they have rights of their own (rather than through a spouse) will be transferred to the Hopis. According to Philip Reno, "Young people growing into maturity find their social status and their role in tribal politics based on their home community. If they relocate they cannot accumulate community status and political roles in a new community" (1978: 3–4). While intrachapter relocation to plots obtained through a homesite lease or to housing estates will enable relocatees to continue participating in chapter and tribal affairs, plots of one-half acre or less are no substitute for a customary use area that extends for miles, one that has religious as well as economic and psychological significance.

The housing estate and community services plan put forth by the Relocation Commission is an interesting concept, but it poses two types of sociocultural problems for Navajo relocatees. First, the housing estate plan will cause conflict with the hosts, both kin and nonkin, unless substantial funds are made available to provide the hosts with comparable benefits. Second, it will lead to conflict between household members and neighbors within the estate because of crowding.

113

The history of the local relocation planning committees that the Relocation Commission has attempted to establish since June 1977 illustrates the need for more active involvement on the part of the host community. As discussed in Chapter 7, the very nature of relocation agencies makes it difficult for them to involve the local people in the planning process. The Relocation Commission tried to overcome this institutional constraint by forming planning committees at the chapter level that would include both relocatees and hosts. In some cases, overzealous staff members "appointed" prominent Navajos to leadership positions on these committees without their knowledge. Nonetheless, committees were formed and met, with attendance encouraged by paying members a $15 stipend per meeting and reimbursing them for travel expenses.

Except for the newly established Big Mountain Planning Committee (Big Mountain is a division of Hard Rock Chapter), by the end of 1978 all these committees had ceased meeting regularly. Many of their members had resigned. The reasons for this failure are complex. They include the expected alienation of any population of potential relocatees from the agency that is trying to remove them, as well as the actions of the tribe's Advisory Council in referring back for further chapter consideration all requests for land withdrawal. The major factor, however, was probably confusion over host involvement in the relocation process.

As seen by the Relocation Commission, a major purpose of the planning committee was to approve the withdrawal of chapter land for housing estates and community facilities. A number of Navajo planning committee members and officials told us that initially they thought these facilities and the housing in the estates would be available for both relocatees and hosts. They thought that in return for withdrawing land they would be able to launch a housing and community development program that would directly benefit all chapter members. When they learned that housing would be for the relocatees alone and that no funds had yet been allocated by Congress for community facilities, they withdrew their support, and the committees ceased to operate effectively. The lesson here is clear: unless relocation plans include substantial benefits for the hosts, it is unreasonable to expect chapters to withdraw scarce lands to meet the housing needs of the relocatees alone.

Housing estates have another disadvantage in that they settle Navajos without wage employment and without customary activities (such as herding) in closer proximity than the large majority are used to. Interestingly enough, over one-third (nine out of twenty-four) of the hosts interviewed referred to this problem when asked, "Do you think it would be good if some of them [potential relocatees] went on to new housing tracts built in chapter centers on the Navajo side of the line in the JUA?" Of the nine respondents, three were worried about the relocatees not being able to have their livestock with them (for this reason, two were doubtful about this option, while one was against it). A fourth felt the option would be a poor one unless the relocatees had jobs: "A family with no future is just problems. People without livestock, older people must have land." As for the remaining five, all felt that the concept of housing estates was contrary to the lifestyle of the Navajos, although one of the five qualified this statement to apply only to "the older and traditional type people." Two others felt estates would interfere with Navajo independence, which is associated with a dispersed settlement pattern. The fourth and fifth went into more detail: "No, there will be a variety of people or relocatees. Each will have certain life experiences. There will be problems living together, and there will be [the] problem of restricted area in which to live. The tracts are going to be confining." And: "That's not a good idea. These people are going to have feuds since a lot of Navajos do not know how to live in a village type settlement. We Navajos are not used to living in confinement." This concern with confinement was also expressed by Navajo Indian Irrigation Project relocatees. When members of over twenty households were asked their reactions to possible relocation to a housing estate, without exception they rejected such an option.

The concern about family conflicts and the confining implications of housing estates is a legitimate one that has plagued a

115

number of government-sponsored settlement schemes around the world. Where people are not accustomed to close neighbors, some become paranoid because they believe that their neighbors are spying on them, while others liken their confinement to being "in jail." It is hard to build a sense of community under such circumstances; rather, minor incidents between children and between adults are magnified, thus contributing to social disorganization. This problem relates both to kin living in the same house and to kin and neighbors in adjacent houses. We have already seen that the building freeze caused conflict when maturing children brought their spouses to live with their parents instead of building separate houses a short distance away. Similar conflicts occurred among District 6 relocatees who lived together at Window Rock, and we can expect the same to happen in housing estates where there is no housing for married children. As for conflict between neighbors, this also happened among the District 6 relocatees at Window Rock, while the five related former JUA families who moved to the same trailer park in St. Johns have been having serious family problems because of their proximity to one other. At the time of the interview, one family had already moved away to the other side of town, while one spouse who had married into the family had separated from her husband. Again, we expect similar conflicts to occur in the Relocation Commission's housing estates.

To date, we are aware of only two former JUA relocatee households that have moved into a rural housing estate that has similarities to those planned by the Relocation Commission. This is a HUD-financed estate of about ten houses built close to the Tolani Lake Chapter headquarters. The housing is of good quality. Members of both households were interviewed. One, an elderly woman who had lived alone in a small hogan in an isolated area, was happy with her new situation because, now that she had a larger house, her daughter and grandchild had come to live with her. This had been impossible before because of the freeze. Her married son, who was employed locally, also lived with her during the week. The other household included a middle-aged couple with their children, three of whom were still at home (one was an infant; two adolescent daughters were bused daily to school). As the following dialogue shows, the unemployed husband was miserable, and both he and his wife regretted moving:

QUESTION: What caused you to move to this place?
ANSWER: We had no assistance in obtaining housing while living in the JUA because of the freeze and when this house was made available we wanted to move in.
QUESTION: What is good about relocation?
ANSWER: At least we got a new house in our own community, but my wife is boss because it is her relatives' land [chapter], not mine, and I am the in-law.
QUESTION: What is bad about relocation?
ANSWER: I feel I should not even participate in chapter meetings anymore because I feel somewhat ashamed that I moved and I no longer have a voice anymore.

There then followed a series of questions about relocation to which the husband replied:

We both feel very hurt about having to move out. That's why we go to the Relocation Commission for more benefits because we feel that it's not worth it. We were told that they would burn our place, but we said "no." . . . At first I said we should not move . . . but our family decided to move, and I left everything to my spouse. Now she wishes that she did not move. Our children want to move back. I tell them to go ahead, but I think they couldn't move back. My wife made the decision to move so she is the head [since the couple now live in her chapter] and I just follow her. . . . We are worse off now because we have to pay for electricity bills and others that we did not pay for before, and we had extra income from our livestock before relocation and now we have none. . . . We feel like we are sitting in jail with no place to go and we are not used to close neighbors. We are not totally comfortable; we cannot even have a Navajo religious ceremony in here like we would in a hogan. . . . We do worry that during the summer

117

[holidays] when other children come home our children [will] get blamed for things other children have
done. We did not have these problems before. We
have gamblers [in the community] which is bad and it
also invites drunks and vehicles. Our children may
get hurt. . . . Their mental state of mind is not like
[it] used to be before; they feel what we feel about relocation, and it frustrates them also. They quarrel
more often, and they reject one another.

QUESTION: Is there anything that has been really hard for you
about this relocation?

ANSWER: Mental depression, nostalgia. And our planning for
our family and future has become almost nonexistent. We just sit and think about what we have
done.

The type of problems and concerns shown by this second
relocatee household, as well as the experience that other low-
income ethnic populations have had with housing estates both in
the United States and elsewhere, have prompted Martin Topper
of the Indian Health Service to state his concern that the housing
estates may "become behavioral sinks populated mostly by older
Navajos living on welfare who have very little to do with their
time and who are cut off from their traditional sheepherding
lifestyles and who have limited access to the traditional psy-
chotherapy of native ceremonies" (1979: 19). Predicting that
relocatees over the age of forty will be "an especially high risk
population," Topper also writes that "it can be estimated from
current data that a good number of these relocation village
residents will become depressed over the prospect of a welfare
existence in high density (for the reservation) housing" (1979:
18).

REDUCTION OF THE INFLUENCE OF THE NAVAJO TRIBAL COUNCIL

For relocation to be effectively carried out, a well-
financed and well-managed relocation agency is required—one
that inevitably will try to expand its effectiveness by increasing
its influence and authority over other agencies with former JUA

responsibilities. This course of action will have a detrimental impact on the efforts of the tribal government to become more self-sufficient according to the current goals and intentions of P.L. 93-638. Should the relocation process continue, the relationship between the tribe, the BIA, and the Relocation Commission should be carefully spelled out so as not to undermine the basis of support for the tribal government. In this regard, we believe that the tribal government should play a leading role in planning former JUA development, with the BIA and the Relocation Commission involved more as executing agencies of whatever plans are formulated for both relocatees and those living on the Navajo side of the partition line.

EXCESSIVE FINANCIAL COSTS

In the case of P.L. 93-531, the costs of implementing the relocation program can conservatively be estimated at $200 million, a sum that can be expected to increase still further if a major effort is made to carry out relocation according to congressional intent. In our opinion, Congress, the American public, and the Navajos could get better value for such an enormous investment if P.L. 93-531 were repealed and replaced with another act of Congress authorizing a major development program for both the Navajo and Hopi residents of the former JUA and for District 6 and Moencopi. Such an approach would benefit all of those involved at a lower financial cost and with less stress. This option is considered in greater detail at the close of this chapter.

UNANTICIPATED PROBLEMS

Unanticipated problems can be expected to accompany programs of compulsory relocation. In the former JUA case, a major unanticipated problem has been the inability of the Navajos to obtain additional land to partially compensate the relocatees for the 900,000 acres that have been partitioned to the Hopis. According to Section 11 of P.L. 93-531, "The Secretary is

119

authorized and directed to transfer not to exceed 250,000 acres of lands under the jurisdiction of the Bureau of Land Management within the States of Arizona or New Mexico to the Navajo Tribe," provided that the tribe pays the fair market value. The law also states that the size of the reservation can be increased through private land purchases by the Navajo tribe provided the total does not exceed 250,000 acres. While the Navajo tribe has identified 250,000 acres under the first category located in the House Rock Valley-Paria Plateau Area, resistance to such a land transfer by a coalition of ranchers and other special interest groups has effectively blocked any action. Although the land in question could absorb only a relatively small number of relocatees, its acquisition has major symbolic importance for the tribal government. The inability of the tribe to acquire additional land has increased the doubts in the minds of potential relocatees about the capacity of their tribal government to represent their interests. Meanwhile, the uncertainty of the relocatees as to where they can go once they are evicted from the former JUA remains.

We believe that these land acquisition problems were not anticipated by Congress. But they exist, and their existence significantly increases the uncertainty surrounding relocation. Colson and Scudder are aware of no major programs of compulsory relocation (aside from those involving war and political refugees) in which potential relocatees have been kept uninformed for so long as to where they would be moved. Should Congress decide to continue the relocation program, we believe that the whole question of land acquisition will have to be rethought and P.L. 93–531 reconsidered in that light.

Amending Public Law 93–531

An amendment to P.L. 93–531 was vetoed by the president of the United States during 1978 primarily because of a modification allowing a one-house veto on any plan submitted by

the Relocation Commission, rather than because of modifica-
tions proposed to ease the stress of relocation for the Navajos.

LIFE ESTATES

The major modification in the 1978 amendment concerned the provision of life estates for relocatees under the
following conditions: (1) The household head or spouse was forty
or over (or disabled). (2) The education and skills of the
household head were considered a barrier to successful relocation in a border town off the reservation. (3) It is not possible
for the household to relocate on the reservation. On such a life
estate, the household would be permitted to keep sufficient
livestock for subsistence purposes and to make improvements
during the tenure of the life estate, which would remain "in
effect until the head of household or spouse died, whichever is
later."

While the concept of a life estate is initially attractive, we are
not convinced that life estates are actually in the interests of
Navajo household heads and spouses over the age of forty. As
written, we see three problems with the life estates provision.

The first problem concerns the difficulty of deciding which
people over the age of forty qualify. What criteria can be identified to establish whether or not a Navajo has the skills to live off
the reservation? The life cycles of people are dynamic, with
major ups and downs. The coping ability of even appropriately
educated people can be seriously compromised by such traumatic
events as divorce, death in the family, or, for that matter, compulsory relocation. An elderly, undereducated Navajo woman
with a more positive attitude toward relocation (perhaps because
it will allow her to join or be closer to her children) may in fact do
better in town than a man with a high school education, job
experience, and/or military service off the reservation who has
decided he prefers life in the former JUA and hence has a negative
attitude toward moving.

Under such circumstances, it will be very difficult to make

judgments about a person's capability to move. For any number of reasons, an apparently capable person may lose that capability shortly after moving. This possibility exists in regard to relocation both on and off the reservation. It is important to remember that the Relocation Commission is already concerned about "the adjustment of approximately 25 percent of the families that have moved off-reservation" (1979). Most of these people have only moved within the past eighteen months. How many more families will have adjustment problems in the years ahead? Furthermore, it is important to understand that these first relocatees tend to be younger and better educated than the larger number of families that still have to relocate. And approximately two-thirds of the first relocatees were already resident or working in town at the time of removal. Yet within a relatively short period of time, 25 percent of this select aggregate of families were having serious adjustment problems. For those still to move, the number of problems and their severity can be expected to be considerably higher.

The second problem concerns the difficulty of determining whether or not relocation is possible on the reservation. We have already explained the difficult position of the tribal government in regard to former JUA relocation, since its credibility will suffer if removal occurs in spite of tribal opposition. Under these circumstances, the tribal government may continue opposing the withdrawal of reservation lands for relocatees. In that event, will this refusal be interpreted to mean that reservation land is not available? If not, then the relocatees' capacity to obtain a life estate will depend on the actions of the tribe rather than on their own needs—which is hardly equitable, granted the lack of influence that the relocatees have on tribal policy.

The third problem is more fundamental and concerns the whole concept of a life estate and its influence on Navajo kinship, the extended family, and the nuclear family. The major problem here is the extent to which life estates will sever the generations and isolate older Navajos from the kinship networks and children on whom they become increasingly dependent as they age. As they grow up and marry, children presumably will be required to move away from parents with life estates: although improvements to the property will be allowed, these will probably not include new housing for former dependents. If this is true, parents will be increasingly separated from their children and younger kin; they will live more and more in isolation. Should children and other kin wish to return for lengthy visits, will this be allowed? And if it is, where will they stay?

The best solution to the first and second problems would be to allow all those over the age of forty to have life estates if they desire them. This, however, does not get at the third problem, which is why repeal of P.L. 93–531 (coupled with a major land acquisition and development program for the Hopis) is considered a more viable alternative than amendment. Short of repeal, there is the option of giving a life estate to everyone born prior to the drawing of the partition line in 1977. While this option might appear to lengthen greatly the period of relocation, there are two reasons why this is not necessarily the case.

First, the existing relocation plan will probably take much longer than was anticipated. Once younger people already living in town have relocated under the new eligibility criteria, the rate of movement under the Relocation Commission's program of "voluntary" relocation may well slow down, especially as potential relocatees learn more about the adjustment problems that at least 25 percent of the present relocatees are having and as the number of relocated elderly people who wish to return increases. Thus we would expect the existing relocation program to continue for another seven years: two more years for plan preparation and five years for the actual relocation program.

Second, giving life estates to everyone born before partition essentially takes the confrontation out of relocation. If such estates were combined with a program of improved education and job training for young people, along with a program generating increased job opportunities elsewhere, one would expect more young people to move out of the area partitioned to the Hopis, either taking their parents with them or moving after their deaths, with depopulation accelerating as more and more people moved.

But this approach also presents difficult problems. Although the freeze on new housing construction and road improvements (designed with eventual Hopi needs in mind) would presumably end, those living on the Hopi side would still be a disadvantaged population, since major development efforts would be carried on elsewhere. No matter how one looks at the life estates approach, there are long-term problems for many of those involved.

LAND ACQUISITION

Granted the tremendous importance of land to the Navajos, and the unexpected problems that have arisen in regard to purchasing additional lands as permitted by P.L. 93–531, the whole question of land acquisition should be reconsidered. Although we were unable to verify the information, we were informed by staff within the BIA, the Navajo tribal government, and the Relocation Commission that there was ample un-occupied, private land for sale surrounding the reservation, especially to the south along Interstate 40. If this is the case, and if relocation is required, we believe that 500,000 to 900,000 acres could be purchased south of the reservation for use by those Navajo relocatees who wish to continue a ranching lifestyle. In its draft plan, the Relocation Commission already intends to do this for the Hopi relocatees: the purchase of over 20,000 acres is being considered for less than one hundred people (Navajo and Hopi Indian Relocation Commission 1978: 138). The equitable thing to do would be to provide the Navajos with a similar option; in this case, up to 900,000 acres would be needed.

Even if land is available, there may be resistance to selling it to the Navajo tribe, especially because of the loss of tax base to local governments. In that case, Congress could appropriate funds to cover such taxes and, if opposition to the land purchase continued, use its condemnation powers. This is necessary because we believe that land purchase is absolutely essential if the intent of Congress to reduce the stresses of relocation is to be realized.

DISTRICT 6 RELOCATEES

All compulsory relocation causes multidimensional stress for the large majority. However, in the Navajo case the impact of eviction has been exceptionally severe for those District 6 relocatees who were moved in 1972. Today many still live under most difficult conditions, having been moved several times, and without having received adequate compensation for their original eviction. Their situation cries out for correction. We believe that the provisions of P.L. 93–531 should be expanded to cover all fifteen households "provided that such heads of households have not already received equivalent assistance from Federal agencies" (H.R.11092 as amended; U.S. Congress 1978c).

DIVISION OF LABOR AND COORDINATION OF ACTIVITIES

Any amendment to P.L. 93–531 will be most effective if it makes explicit the division of labor between the Navajo tribal government, the Relocation Commission, the BIA, and the other major agencies with former JUA relocation responsibilities. It must also come to grips with problems of coordination and consider the establishment of an oversight mechanism, possibly responsible directly to Congress. Without proper coordination and oversight, the relocatees will suffer as agencies vie with one another for influence and funds. On the other hand, what mechanisms for coordination are established must be carefully thought out so that they do not infringe on the influence and authority of the Navajo tribal government contrary to the intent of the Indian Self-Determination Act.

COMMUNITY FACILITIES AND ECONOMIC DEVELOPMENT

At the very least, adequate funds should be appropriated to provide community facilities and social services to the relocatees, and to finance research for planning purposes and experimental pilot approaches to both relocation and development. While the Relocation Commission has included community facilities in its preliminary plan, no funds are available to finance them. Nor are funds available to improve counseling for relocatees before, during, and after relocation on a family-by-family and workshop basis. As for development, no authorization exists for undertaking appropriate research for planning purposes, for creating job training centers, or for undertaking pilot projects. In authorizing such activities (with sufficient sums appropriated for their execution), Congress would be well advised to specify, in regard to their planning and execution, the relationship between the Navajo tribal government, the Relocation Commission, and other relevant agencies in keeping with the intent of the Indian Self-Determination Act.

Repeal of Public Law 93–531

This option has three major advantages and one major disadvantage. The advantages are the following: (1) It greatly reduces the human costs for at least 5,000 potential Navajo relocatees. (2) It is financially the least expensive option. (3) It is more consistent with United States policy in regard to the Indian Self-Determination Act, in regard to other Indian land claims, and in regard to human rights in domestic and international affairs. The major disadvantage is that repeal does not come to grips with legitimate Hopi claims unless it is accompanied by a major Hopi development plan that includes funds and mechanisms for the acquisition of new lands, for job training, and for the creation of additional employment opportunities.

ADVANTAGES

The human and financial costs of relocation have already been discussed. We have also discussed the destabilizing effects that a massive relocation program will have on the Navajo tribal government, contrary to the intent of the Indian Self-Determination Act. Elsewhere Indian land claims, especially those in New England between Indians and others, have been settled through cash compensation to the Indian authorities rather than through massive relocation of non-Indians. Repeal also has the advantage of eliminating a potentially embarrassing situation for the United States since a strong argument can be made that compulsory relocation violates the human rights of the relocatees, contrary to United States policy.

DISADVANTAGES

Land is also of tremendous importance to the Hopis, especially the land that surrounds the inhabited mesas both within the former JUA and around Moencopi. The Navajo and Hopi situations differ, however, in regard to one major factor: partition of former JUA lands and of land surrounding Moencopi will require the compulsory relocation of thousands of Navajos, while retention of those lands by the Navajos will require no forced relocation of Hopis. (Those Hopis living in the Jeddito Island, who number less than one hundred, could be allowed to remain in the area as a condition of repeal.) Such retention will cause other hardship to the Hopis, however, so that repeal of P.L. 93-531 should be linked with a major program to counteract current and expected hardships.

It is unlikely that the Hopi Tribal Council will voluntarily accept any congressional decision that allows the Navajos to remain on the land that has been partitioned to the Hopis, regardless of other compensation offered. This is understandable—just as understandable as the present resistance of the Navajos to partition. In other words, it is unlikely that Congress will be able to come up with any solution that will have the support of both parties to the dispute. However, every effort should be made to discuss alternative solutions with both the Hopi Tribal Council and the leaders and members of each of the Hopi villages. Only in that way can a settlement be reached that will attempt to meet the very real and diverse needs of the Hopi people, of their village leaders, and of their tribal representatives. While we do not know what these specific needs are, what little contact we have had with both the former JUA and Moencopi land disputes suggests that there has been a tendency to oversimplify their nature. Conditions in certain Hopi villages are overcrowded, and land for expansion is needed both in the Moencopi and District 6 cases. This land is needed not just for farming and cattle ranching but for the establishment of new village sites and housing areas. While the need is very great, we repeat once again that it does not justify the massive relocation of thousands of Navajos who have lived on the land in question for generations—at least 5,000 Navajos in the case of the land currently partitioned to the Hopis in the former JUA and several thousand Navajos in the case of the Hopi claims in the Moencopi area.

Hopi needs do justify linking repeal of P.L. 93–531 with an act of Congress that would include such goals as the following: (1) Mechanisms for the funding and acquisition of up to 900,000 acres between the southern boundary of the Navajo Reservation and Interstate 40, suitable not just for ranching but also for locating new Hopi villages. While such lands are not adjacent to District 6, it is important to point out that they are not much further away than Moencopi is from District 6. Furthermore, their proximity to Interstate 40 could open up a number of development opportunities. (2) Hopi access to a proportion of jobs and opportunities associated with the ongoing development of Tuba City. (3) Access to land for housing in the Tuba City area, provided such access does not require the eviction of Navajo households. (4) Preparation of an integrated development plan for the Hopi people. (5) Execution of education, job training, and development programs to upgrade skills and provide an increasing number and range of economic opportunities for the Hopi people.

These goals are merely suggestions. As previously mentioned, the actual assessment of needs, and all attempts to meet them, should be a joint, federally funded effort, with Hopi involvement at all levels in the identification of needs and goals, and in the planning, implementation, management, and evaluation of programs designed to meet those needs.

Epilogue

JERRY KAMMER and THAYER SCUDDER

This epilogue consists of two parts. Intentionally distinct, they present the current views of an experienced journalist (Kammer) and a social scientist (Scudder) on the land dispute. Part One contains reflections by Kammer, the author of *The Second Long Walk: The Navajo-Hopi Land Dispute* (1980). Part Two, by Scudder, is an update of the history of the land dispute and its impact upon the Navajo residents of the former Joint Use Area since March 1979.

Part One: A Journalist's View

In Arthur Miller's classic American drama *Death of a Salesman,* the wife of Willy Loman cries out for recognition of the tragedy that is quietly destroying her husband. "Attention!" she demands. "Attention must finally be paid . . ." (Act I).

About 100 miles east of the Grand Canyon, in the high desert rangeland of northeastern Arizona, a tragedy of far greater proportions is underway. This tragedy, too, is unfolding without the public attention and concern that might avert it. There the United States government has begun a program to relocate at least 6,000 Navajos from land it has awarded to the Hopi tribe. The relocation program, the largest forced removal of Indians in a century, will add a tragic, ignoble, and wholly unnecessary chapter to the history of this country's Indian affairs.

A large body of evidence, of which this study is an important

part, demonstrates that when Congress authorized the relocation program in 1974 it did not understand the implications of
expelling traditional Indians from the land that is their only
source of stability in a world of seismic cultural upheaval. It has
also become clear that this program, which will be carried out at
enormous cost in human suffering and in federal tax dollars, will
benefit few Hopis.

But while the evidence is impressive, Congress refuses to be
impressed. It refuses to pay more than the required token
attention. In early July 1981 the few members of the House and
Senate involved with Indian matters accepted a vague and
frequently evasive plan developed by the Navajo and Hopi Indian
Relocation Commission. A five-year period was thus begun
during which relocation is to be completed. Most Navajos will
doubtlessly move from their land, bending to the relentless will
of the law from Washington, even as it breaks their spirit. Others
will remain, waiting for the federal marshalls.

Few members of Congress have ever taken more than a casual
look at this frequently complex struggle for land between two
Indian tribes off in a dusty corner of Arizona. And so the
legislation that sought to resolve the Navajo-Hopi dispute has
been shaped by a handful of senators and representatives. One of
the most important figures in Indian affairs today is Morris Udall
of Arizona, chairman of the House Interior Committee. Udall
voted against relocation in 1974 but now says P.L. 93–531 was
passed "after long deliberation and careful consideration"
(Kammer 1980: 169) and insists that the Hopi victory it
represents must be defended. Arizona U.S. Senator Dennis
DeConcini's advocacy of repeal of the relocation legislation and
substitution of financial compensation for the Hopis offends
Udall's sense of fair play. Udall regards the idea as the political
equivalent of an athletic team seeking to replay a game it has lost.

In his public utterances, at least, Udall is sanguine about
relocation. "Once the people who have to move accept the fact
that they have to move, all these relocation problems become
very easy," he said. "We've got generous assistance for them. It's
kind of a psychological thing. After the first four families move,

131

the next group will be able to move a lot more easily" (Kammer 1980: 171).

In the face of stark evidence to the contrary, Udall's optimism is wishful thinking. As the Relocation Commission itself has reported, some of the Navajos who have already moved are adjusting poorly. And these are primarily the young, educated, and culturally mobile, who were eager to take advantage of the relocation benefits. When the older Navajos, most of whom do not speak English, are forced to relocate—those who have lived only the life of the land, extended family, and livestock—the failure rate will climb drastically and this "generous" federal program will likely become a national disgrace.

Most of the Navajos marked for relocation continue to cling tenaciously to the land, like the hardy desert plants that somehow draw sustenance from it. They are hoping that sometime over the next five years Congress will reconsider what it has done and allow them time to stay. "They have a lot of faith in justice, even though it's not being given to them," said tribal councilman David Clark. Clark said the relocation program is causing "tremendous strain" among his people:

> They just break down and cry while I'm talking with them. All you have to do is touch it and it comes out. One of the expressions I hear a lot is that the government is tearing their hearts out while they're still alive. They say, "I'm not an animal. I'm not a prisoner. But that's the way I'm being treated in my own country."

The Navajos call the law for relocation "Bilagáana Bibee-haz'áanii," the white man's law. They say it is violating their own natural and religious laws that sanction their life on the land, where many of them still pray to the springs and trees and sprinkle corn pollen in the morning to receive the benediction of the Dawn People. "The people have lived all their lives there," said one Navajo. "The land is sacred to them. It's like an altar to them. They don't see any reason for them to move."

When the five-year relocation period runs out in 1986, the possibility for violence is clearly great. One Navajo told the *New*

132

York Times in 1977 that if a federal marshall comes to evict him, "I'll shoot the hell out of that bastard." There have already been several incidents of violent resistance to the federal program that is reducing Navajo livestock and fencing off the partitioned land. In 1978 an agitated Navajo woman fired a rifle shot over the heads of a fence crew. Last fall, in an attempt to block construction of the fence along the new Navajo-Hopi border, an elderly Navajo woman and her three daughters fought with BIA police, whose behavior on the disputed land has often been erratic and reckless. The women were maced, thrown to the ground, handcuffed, and hauled away. In May 1981 millions of Americans received an introduction to the passions of the land dispute in a brief ABC news report that showed a young Navajo woman slapping the face of a BIA official directing the impoundment of Navajo stock on the Hopi partition area. "See what you did to my people; see what you did to them!" she screamed.

The tension in the area is palpable. One measure of the mood of the Navajos living on the Hopi partition area is the stories of Navajo veterans stockpiling weapons. Some of the veterans are openly defiant. "What they'll have to do if they want me to move is move my carcass," said Roger Attakai, army veteran and president of the Teesto Chapter. "I ain't leaving this place. My roots are way down in the land, and my feeling for living is in it, too." Veterans feel a particularly acute grievance at being forced from the land by Washington, and others look to them for leadership.

Morris Udall's defense of the relocation legislation as the product of long deliberation and careful consideration does not stand up to an examination of Congress' handling of the land dispute. Had Congress looked into the dispute, it would have learned that Representative Sam Steiger (a key sponsor of the relocation legislation) was wrong when he said a decision to reject relocation and buy out the Hopi interest in the disputed land "would constitute a blanket endorsement of economic and cultural genocide of our country's oldest surviving Indian tribe" (Kammer 1980:115). It would have learned that Steiger was an important part in an artful but artificial Hopi public relations

133

campaign that warned of war unless relocation was enacted, suggesting that the Arizona range would be set aflame by the passions of two seething tribal foes.

A congressional investigating team would have learned that relations between the two tribes are for the most part coopera- tive and cordial. It would have learned that many Hopis do not want to see the Navajos removed and that the tribal council is not representative of the tribe as a whole. The Navajos marked for relocation do not represent a threat to the Hopi culture. Instead they represent a threat to what might be called the new Hopi elite, most of whom are affluent and eager to expand their cattle herds. Hopi-Tewa Albert Yava raises this central issue in his autobiographical work *Big Falling Snow:*

> The well-off Hopi has special interests. If he owns a lot of cattle, for example, that land we have been contesting with the Navajos is much more important to him than to a poor family in [the village of] Shipaulovi. The average Hopi isn't going to benefit very much from the land settlement. [1978: 125]

But there was no study, no investigating team, no critical analysis of the testimony of the Hopi chairman that he repre- sented a vulnerable David being stomped upon by the Navajo Goliath. Congress simply collected the testimony of the two sides at formal hearings—which provide an inadequate forum for understanding an issue as complex as this—and with brief token visits to the disputed lands. The legislative process as it was applied to the land dispute failed Theodore White's definition of politics as "the slow public application of reason to the governing of mass emotion." That process was truncated and manipulated by a handful of poorly informed legislators and by a Hopi lobbying and public relations compaign that successfully propa- gated the David and Goliath myth. The real underdogs in this dispute are the traditional Navajos whose way of life is being terminated by congressional fiat. This is now clear. But unless Congress chooses to see it, it is nothing more than a prosaic, futile observation.

The unconscionability of Congress' failure to probe the land dispute carefully before passing legislation to resolve it is highlighted by a comparison with the magnitude of the government's response to the Navajo attempt in 1975 to purchase land for the relocatees. The contrast betrays a clear and odious double standard.

The 1974 Navajo and Hopi Land Settlement Act had promised the Navajos the right to buy up to a quarter of a million acres of federal land as partial compensation for the 911,000 acres they would be forced to leave as a result of partition. But when the Navajos said they wanted to buy land administered by the Bureau of Land Management north of the Grand Canyon, they ran smack into a politically well-connected coalition of hunters, ranchers, and environmentalists who wanted to keep the land in the public domain.

Responding to pressure from the coalition's allies in Congress, Secretary of the Interior Thomas Kleppe ordered an environmental impact statement on prospective Navajo settlement of the area. A special federal task force finished this statement more than three years later at a cost of hundreds of thousands of dollars. Congress then passed legislation in 1980 specifically prohibiting Navajo purchase of the land.

Another example of the lack of congressional insight into the dispute was the life estates program enacted in 1980 to ease the trauma of relocation. The new legislation authorized ninety-acre life estates for up to 120 Navajo families living on Hopi land. But the Navajos have since repudiated the idea of living on small fenced-off islands within land from which their relatives have been removed. It turns out that the concept of life estates cannot even be translated into Navajo. Indeed, with a perverse irony, the idea comes across in Navajo metaphysics as "death estates" (see Wood et al. 1981: 20).

A young Navajo explained. "When you implant something in someone's mind, you cause it to happen," said Roman Bitsuie, a Princeton graduate now working for the tribe's land-dispute commission. "So with life estates, in essence what we'd have to say is, 'You're going to die.'" Sandra Massetto, a member of the Relocation Commission, told the Senate Select Committee on

135

Indian Affairs why the Navajos are not applying for the life estates. "They are concerned life estates will separate them from their families and they will be left to die. . . . I frankly don't think it is an alternative they are interested in."

What the Navajos remain interested in as an alternative to relocation is a buy-out of the Hopi partition area. And it must be said again and again that the decision by Congress not to order a buy-out is the most serious example of a legal double standard in the turbulent history of the land dispute. For in previous land disputes involving settlers on land recognized by courts as belonging to Indian tribes the settlers have been non-Indian, and the government has intervened by providing financial compensation for the tribes and allowing the settlers to remain. An attorney for the Navajos made the point succinctly in 1974, when he asked Congress, "Could it be, may I ask, that where the settlers are white, we pay off the original owners in cash, but where the settlers are Indian, we find expulsion and removal an acceptable alternative? Can such a racially discriminatory approach be considered as meeting the constitutional requirement of due process?" (Kammer 1980: 99). The question still demands an answer.

Another point that merits careful consideration during this five-year countdown to final relocation is the possible role of energy interests in the 1974 legislation. The Navajos who must relocate insist that the underlying motivation for partition and relocation is a desire to get at the huge coal deposits that underlie much of the land the Navajos must leave. Their position gains credibility from the fact that two former federal employees who pushed hard for relocation—a high-ranking Interior Department official and a former staff director of the Senate Interior Committee—are now vice-presidents of energy companies that have long had their eye on Navajo and Hopi energy resources. The suggestion of a possible conflict of interests on the part of these two men is part of the large body of information on the land dispute now available that would justify a complete reopening of the federal program to resolve the Navajo-Hopi dispute.

The French historian Alexis de Tocqueville, who witnessed

what he called the "solemn spectacle" of the Choctaw forced migration beyond the Mississippi in 1831, was struck by the ability of the advancing whites to deprive Indians of their rights and wipe them out "with singular felicity, tranquilly, legally, philanthropically, without shedding blood, and without violating a single great principle of morality in the eyes of the world" (de Tocqueville 1945: 352-53, 364). The program to relocate thousands of Navajos is a tragic and ultimately unjustifiable departure from the admirable spirit of recent decades, when the federal government has supported tribal governments and cultures. In its callousness to human suffering and in its grounding in a double standard of justice, it is a repetition of the history recorded by de Tocqueville. It is a reinvocation of the mean spirited time of the Trail of Tears and the Navajos' own Long Walk.

If there is bloodshed in 1986, it is certain that attention will finally be paid to this new Indian Tragedy—not only by media always eager for stories of Indians on the warpath, but by the entire world. Then the relocation program may well become not only a national disgrace but an international embarrassment. At that point Congress would have little choice but to reexamine what it is doing in northeastern Arizona to one of the last traditional peoples in the United States.

Part Two: A Social Scientist's View

On April 18, 1979, the U.S. District Court for Arizona confirmed the boundary partitioning the former JUA between the Hopi and Navajo people. From that date, as directed by P.L. 93-531, the Navajo and Hopi Indian Relocation Commission had two years to prepare and submit a relocation report to Congress. The following year Congress passed the Navajo and Hopi Indian Relocation Amendments Act of 1980 (P.L. 96-305), which authorized the Secretary of the Interior to transfer up to 250,000 acres of land under the jurisdiction of the Bureau of Land Management (BLM) to the Navajo tribe and to accept the title on behalf of the United States of up to 150,000 acres of private land purchased by the Navajo tribe as partial replacement for the 911,000 acres partitioned to the Hopi tribe. None of this land can be north and west of the Colorado River (hence restricting the Navajos from acquiring the House Rock Valley and Paria Plateau BLM land which had been their first choice), and in all cases at least one border must be within eighteen miles of an existing boundary of the Navajo Reservation.

Since much of this land is checkerboarded (pieces of BLM land alternate with private or state-owned land), the amending legislation will make it more difficult for the government to acquire replacement land. While land exchanges will be necessary to put together areas large enough for relocation purposes, purchases will be difficult, since the Secretary of the Interior is authorized by Congress to exchange such lands only if the purchase price of the private lands does not exceed the appraised value of BLM lands by 25 percent. As Gary Verburg, attorney for the Navajo Nation, pointed out in congressional testimony on May 20, 1981:

> The Navajo Tribe is in a "catch-22" situation. On the one hand, it can only acquire lands within eighteen miles, driving the asking price for such lands up to 200 percent or 300 percent of the land's fair market value. On the other hand, BLM can only exchange lands for consolidation purposes up to 125 percent of the value of the private lands being exchanged. [Verburg 1981:3]

Under these and previous circumstances, it is hardly surprising that no major land purchases have yet been arranged in spite of the fact that P.L. 93–531 was passed over six years ago.

On April 18, 1981, the Relocation Commission submitted its report and plan to Congress. Though hearings held before the Senate Select Committee on Indian Affairs on May 20 pointed out very serious deficiencies within the plan, Congress took no further action. The plan therefore became law in mid-July—ninety days after its submission, as stipulated in P.L. 93–531. Throughout this period the Relocation Commission has continued to move families under its "voluntary" relocation program, with 331—approximately 12 percent of the households claiming residence on the Hopi side of the partition line—moved through June 1981. As in the past, these relocatees continue to be unrepresentative of the majority to be moved in the future if relocation continues, since they tend to be relatively young and educated, with 75 percent of the household heads already living off the reservation at the time of their removal (and not infrequently already residing temporarily in their preferred relocation site).

As the federal government presses ahead with the relocation program, it is obvious that Congress continues to seriously underestimate the disadvantages of compulsory relocation as a solution to the tragic and long-standing Navajo-Hopi land dispute. Underestimation relates especially to the magnitude of the human costs for the relocatees, the number of relocatees, and the financial costs of their removal.

In 1974 testimony before the Senate Committee on Interior and Insular Affairs, I predicted that relocation of Navajos would cause death rates to rise. I also stated that "those responsible for programs of compulsory relocation tend to underestimate the capital costs by a factor of two to three . . . and they underestimate the number of people requiring relocation." As we shall see, capital costs have in fact been underestimated by more than a factor of four, and the number of potential Navajo relocatees may be more than double the original estimate of 3,500.

THE HUMAN COSTS OF RELOCATION

Throughout the testimony before Congress during the 1970s, expert witness after witness testified to the extremely detrimental impacts of relocation for a people like the Navajo with strong economic, social, political, and religious ties to their land. To the best of my knowledge, no expert has argued that relocation is not extremely stressful, while hundreds of traditional Navajos have told countless officials, journalists, and researchers what their land means to them while reiterating their conviction that some Navajos will die from the stress of removal from that land (see Appendix 3). The accuracy of these forecasts already appears to be borne out by the ongoing relocation program, although in the absence of controlled scientific research it is not possible to prove conclusively that the apparent rise in Navajo death rates among those living on the Hopi side of the partition line is due to the land dispute.

We have recounted in detail throughout this book the adverse effects of relocation for the Navajo and people like the Navajo. Since the original report was submitted, further research (some of which is published and some not) sponsored by such agencies as the Indian Health Service, the Navajo and Hopi Indian Relocation Commission, the Big Mountain Community, the National Endowment for the Humanities, and the U.S. Environmental Protection Agency has confirmed or duplicated our results, while no research has suggested that they are exaggerated, let alone incorrect.

In a July 1980 report to the Indian Health Service, Martin Topper, an Indian Health Service employee, wrote that the stress associated with the land dispute is becoming "heavier" for the Navajo, with those over the age of forty and with less than 5.5 years of education a high-risk population. Scudder, he notes, "predicted that these would be high risk groups for the development of stress, and the data of patients of the Navajo Area Mental Health Branch has provided evidence for his opinion" (Topper 1980: 24). Within the former JUA, "Navajos about to be relocated are still using Navajo Area mental health services at a rate which is 4.26 times that of JUA Navajos who will not be relocated" (p. 1). For those relocated off the reservation, Topper refers to Relocation Commission staff reports that 25 percent are failing to make a successful adjustment to removal. Furthermore, "13 percent of relocated Navajo families were in the process of selling their off-reservation homes and were attempting to return to the reservation" (p. 2). Here it must be remembered that most of the off-reservation families to which

Topper is referring are younger and better educated than the large majority yet to be moved.

In their final report to the Environmental Protection Agency, Schoepfle and his colleagues (April 1981) discuss the results of research which included interviews with potential Navajo relocatees from the former JUA and with other Navajos relocated in connection with the Navajo Indian Irrigation Project. Many Navajos, they reported, summed up relocation as meaning "the end of life: and that was that. Others simply said that they were worse off, and some said that while they themselves may have benefitted from improved jobs, those around them did not" (Schoepfle et al. 1981: 24). In an earlier report dealing with potential former JUA Navajo relocatees from Teesto Chapter, these researchers reported Navajo convictions that "many elderly people have passed on because of the dispute" (Schoepfle et al. 1980: 29).

Recent research by John Wood and his colleagues details the effects of the Navajo-Hopi land dispute on Navajo well-being at Big Mountain. A respected researcher, Wood had previously been hired to undertake research in the former JUA by both the Bureau of Indian Affairs and the Navajo and Hopi Indian Relocation Commission. In a 1981 report to Congress, he and his colleagues wrote, "People at Big Mountain are striving to meet their needs, but they are very frustrated: tears were not unusual in interviews we took . . . and there have been many deaths recently, attributed to the effects of the land dispute" (Wood et al. 1981: 15). Moreover,

> the passage of P.L. 93–531 has placed unending hardships on the Navajos of Big Mountain, both physically and psychologically. If the blame for such events is to be placed on any shoulders, then it must be placed on our government's one hundred years of inactivity, misconceptions, and varied interests in the area. . . . Governmental action has also infringed upon peoples' free exercise of religion as it is stated in the First Amendment. Big Mountain is considered sacred among the Navajo who live in and around this area . . . . It is a

> focal point and a reminder to the Navajos of the Holy People who set this area aside for them. [P. 21]

Indeed, Wood et al. maintain that by forcing the Big Mountain people to leave Congress is "also forcing them to leave behind their religion" (p. 20) contrary to the intent of P.L. 95–341 (The American Indian Religious Freedom Act). Though Big Mountain is sacred beyond its boundaries, Navajos living in other former JUA chapters feel no differently about their land; as Wood et al. state, "land and religion are synonymous to the Navajo people" (p. 22).

In spite of such studies and testimony, with no contrary opinions voiced by knowledgeable experts, the Congress of the United States has ignored the warnings and proceeded with a program of relocation which violates the religious freedom of the Navajos, deprives them of livelihood, subjects them to great emotional stress, and can be expected to increase death rates among the relocatees.

THE NUMBER OF NAVAJOS TO BE RELOCATED

Over the years estimates of the number of potential relocatees have risen significantly. The original estimate was 3,500. The Relocation Commission raised this to 4,800 in its December 1978 Interim Progress Report and to 5,600 during 1979. In its April 1981 Report and Plan, however, the Relocation Commission stated that 2,801 Navajo households, comprised of 9,525 Navajos, live on land partitioned to the Hopis. Though the Commission estimates that only 1,540 families (or approximately 6,850 people, of whom slightly over 100 are Hopis) will actually qualify for relocation benefits, no attempt is made to justify this estimate in the report. This too is probably an underestimate. Even if it is not, according to the 1980 U.S. Census, the number of Navajos now to be relocated exceeds the entire population of Hopis currently living in District 6.

FINANCIAL COSTS OF THE RELOCATION PLAN

Current relocation costs according to the 1981 Report and Plan of the Relocation Commission come to nearly $200 million—roughly four times the amount authorized for appropriation under P.L. 93-531. While such a sum is necessary if the intent of Congress is to be carried out in terms of housing and social services, this sum does not include funds for job training and other essential components of a development program. Study after study around the world has shown that while housing and social services are important, the most important single component of a relocation program is economic opportunity, in the form of land and jobs that enable the relocatees to support themselves after removal.

As Aberle pointed out in his May 1981 testimony to the Senate Select Committee on Indian Affairs, not only is the relocation Commission's plan expensive, but it is also "unworkable." Neither Congress nor the Navajo Nation has been informed where people will be moved to, in spite of the tremendous significance of land to the Navajos.

> The Tribe's first choice, House Rock Valley and Paria Plateau, was refused to them. The Report lists other possible lands, but that is not a plan. . . . Selection of new lands is still ahead, their development lies beyond that. . . . There is no estimate of costs. So far as I know, there is no allocation of funds for development. [Aberle 1981: 5]

The cost of acquiring land is not included in the Relocation Commission's report. Also omitted are costs for the increased needs for health care, welfare, and general assistance which are expected to follow when Navajos are relocated to housing estates with no jobs and no land. When all the direct and indirect costs of carrying out P.L. 93-531 as amended are added together, economic consultants to the Navajo tribe (including Stanford Research Institute International) have estimated that the total costs may exceed half a billion dollars. Even then success for the majority of the relocatees is not ensured. As we have recommended, it would be more economical in terms of human and financial costs to repeal P.L. 93–531 and to replace it with a development program for both the Navajo residents of the former JUA and the Hopis—a recommendation with which Wood et al. agree (1981: 21). Not only would such a program cost less, but it would benefit more people. As Aberle concludes, the present plan "requires hundreds of millions of dollars to relocate a very large number of American Indians, mostly Navajos, to nonexistent places to do nonexistent things. It is a recipe perhaps for violence and certainly for grief and poverty" (Aberle 1981: 8–9).

Furthermore, there is a major risk that the enormous costs of nonproductive relocation will be used in the future as an argument by government officials to allocate less money for productive purposes than might otherwise be the case. And Hopi needs, which are also very real, can be met through other mechanisms. In fact, much of the land that the Navajos are required to vacate under the present law will not be settled by Hopis, but will be used for cattle ranching by a relatively small number of Hopi families. Grazing land for cattle can be found elsewhere without the removal of over 6,000 people being required. Indeed, as we have said, the purchase of substitute land for the Hopis, along with a joint development program, would cost less than the current relocation program.

According to P.L. 93–531, relocation should be carried out in such a way as to "avoid or minimize, to the extent possible," adverse social, economic, cultural and other inpacts (U.S. Congress 1974: 7). That very wording illustrates the extent to which Congress has underestimated the adverse effects of compulsory relocation, since no such programs can be carried out without adverse effects. Even to minimize such effects requires a major development program of a sort which Congress to date has not considered. Under the present circumstances it is literally impossible to carry out relocation according to the intent of this wording, and there is no evidence to suggest that the necessary funds will be allocated during the 1980s.

In closing I would like to raise the question of why Congress has pursued a course of action which does such violence to the most fundamental rights of one of the poorest and most defenseless populations in the United States. Kammer has touched on possible explanations, including the deference of Congress to the Arizona "expertise" of Morris Udall, who backs the compulsory relocation of over 6,000 Navajos. Kammer places special emphasis on inadequate congressional attention paid to the causes of the land dispute, to the choice of an option involving massive relocation, and to the adverse impacts of such relocation on people like the Navajo. Throughout this history of this dispute, greater attention has been paid to the statements of tribal councils and their attorneys and public relations firms than to the beliefs and feelings of the people most directly involved— the Navajos and Hopis who actually live within the former JUA. At the same time, virtually no attention has been paid to the allegations of many Navajos that relocation is being pushed by those who hope to gain access to the extensive coal and uranium resources that underlie parts of the former JUA and that obviously would be easier to mine if people did not live on top of them.

It may be that Congress has continued to downplay the impacts of forced relocation partly because, as highly educated, mobile people, congressmen regard relocation as "no big deal"; if they think about the issues involved at all, they tend to downplay them. Here they overlook the price that they themselves may be paying for mobility. People in the United States are constantly on the move as they seek out better job opportunities. They assume that moving voluntarily from one locale to another is not stressful for themselves and for members of their families, but they are wrong. According to Weissman and Paykel (1972):

> The evidence from our clinical experience, though anecdotal, suggests that moves in modern America tend to be far more stressful than cultural expectations will permit them to be viewed . . . but the moves are in fact laden with stress. These stresses can try the individual's adaptive abilities beyond capacity and can result in long-term feelings of powerlessness and despair. [P. 19]

145

Though their evidence relates primarily to women, the authors go on to state that "we believe that moving also creates stresses for men—and that its impact extends well beyond the narrow bounds of the depression clinic or of any social class. It is, in fact, a stress that is extremely common, though ignored or underestimated, in American society today" (p. 16).

In their article, Weissman (who is currently an associate professor of Psychiatry and Epidemiology at the Yale University School of Medicine) and Paykel are discussing voluntary moves, not the compulsory relocation of poorly educated Navajos whose present and future well-being is dependent on continued access to their land—land which the Congress of the United States has chosen to take away from them. Killian (1970) has noted how death rates among elderly people moved from one custodial care center to another tend to go up following their removal. The same can be expected among elderly Navajos and among younger Navajo women for the reasons dealt with exhaustively in this report; indeed it would appear that death rates already are increasing among potential relocatees. Congress has legislated an option which not only violates the human rights of these people but which also threatens their lives.

Institutional Affiliations and Names of Officials and Scholars Contacted by the Research Team

University of Arizona
  Professor Jerrold E. Levy

Bureau of Indian Affairs, Flagstaff Office
  Mr. William Benjamin, Director
  Mr. Lynn Montgomery

California State University, Northridge
  Dr. Richard O. Clemmer

University of California, Irvine
  Professor Joseph Jorgensen

Indian Health Service, Navajo Area Public Health Service,
Department of Health, Education and Welfare
  Dr. Marlene E. Haffner, Director
  Mr. Boyd Endischee
  Mr. William Stapleton
  Dr. Martin Topper

Navajo and Hopi Indian Relocation Commission
  Mr. Hawley Atkinson, Commissioner
  Mr. Roger K. Lewis, Commissioner
  Ms. Sandra L. Massetto, Commissioner
  Mr. Leon H. Berger, Executive Director
  Ms. Vicki Cunningham
  Mr. David Shaw
  Mr. Paul Tessler
  Mr. David Williams

Navajo Community College, Shiprock
  Mr. Johnny John
  Ms. Rose T. Morgan
  Mr. Philip Reno
  Mr. G. Mark Schoepfle
  Mr. Henry Thomas

Navajo Nation, Chairman's Office
  Mr. Samuel Pete

Navajo Nation, Department of Economic Development
  Mr. Al Henderson, Director

Navajo Nation, Information Services Department
  Dr. Ronald G. Faich, Director

Navajo Nation, Land Administration Department
  Mr. Charles Morrison
  Mr. R. Scrivner
  Ms. E. Shorty
  Mr. Edison Woods

Navajo Nation, Legal Department
  Mr. Michael V. Stuhff

Navajo Office of Veterans Affairs
  Mr. Gibson B. Jones, Acting Director

Navajo Paralegal Training Program
  Mr. Jerry Kammer, Consultant

Navajo Tribal Council
  Mr. Victor Beck, Land Dispute Commissioner
  Mr. David Clark, Land Dispute Commissioner
  Mr. Joe Dayzie, Land Dispute Commissioner
  Mr. Raymond Gilmore, Black Mesa Review Board
  Mr. Freddie Howard, Land Dispute Commissioner
  Mr. Emmett Tso, Land Dispute Commissioner

Navajo-Hopi Land Dispute Commission
  Mr. Marlin E. Scott, Sr., Former Chairman
  Mr. Percy Deal, Executive Director
  Mr. Emmett Lefthand, Assistant Director

Mr. Leon Begay
Mr. Dale Pete

Museum of Northern Arizona
  Dr. Hermann K. Bleibtreu, Director

Northern Arizona University
  Dr. Walter M. Vannette
  Dr. John J. Wood

University of Notre Dame
  Professor Tom T. Sasaki

Vlassis, Ruzow & Crowder, Phoenix
  Ms. Katherine Ott
  Mr. Lawrence A. Ruzow
  Mr. George P. Vlassis

Classification of Interview Respondents

JOHN WILLIAMSON

A major goal of this report has been to identify background characteristics such as age, sex, and education that are associated with successful relocation. We assumed that it is possible, upon examination of sufficient evidence, to sensibly classify relocatees as adjusting well to relocation, adjusting poorly, or falling somewhere in between. Respondents were classified by a panel of three consisting of Cynthia Carlson, Thayer Scudder, and John Williamson. Carlson and Williamson are graduate students in economics at the California Institute of Technology and have had no previous contact with the Navajo tribe or knowledge of the Navajo-Hopi land dispute. Thus it was expected that they would not exaggerate the problems of the respondents; indeed, before reading the interviews both Carlson and Williamson were skeptical about the rigors of relocation.

After agreeing not to consult with one another until the classifications were complete, each panel member was instructed to read the interviews of 47 of the 48 relocatees in the sample (the forty-eighth interview was incomplete) and classify each respondent as a good, mixed, or poor coper. In arriving at this judgment of overall relocation success, the members were instructed to consider any information a respondent might have supplied about the other members of his household who had relocated with him. However, when making decisions, the panel members were told to ignore information concerning problems common to all people and not specifically related to relocation. After the classifications were completed, they were aggregated into a single measure of relocation success, which was employed in the analysis contained in the body of the study. If all three members agreed on a respondent's classification, the matter was considered settled. In those cases in which only two members agreed, their judgment prevailed. If all three panel members disagreed, a classification of mixed was assigned.

Panel members expected that their classifications would exhibit considerable disagreement. Surprisingly, this was not the case. The panel was in unanimous agreement in 29 out of the 47 cases (62 percent). As for the remaining cases, at least two panel members agreed in 17 cases (36 percent), while in only a single instance did all three panel members disagree. Further, in all 17 cases in which two panel members agreed, the third member's judgment was only one category distant from the majority opinion. There were no instances in which two members classified a respondent as a good coper while the third member classified the same respondent as a poor coper. Conversely, there were no instances in which two members classified a respondent as a poor coper while the third panel member judged the same respondent as a good coper. The panel's judgment concerning those respondents classified as poor copers was largely undivided: 14 of 18 respondents classified as poor copers were so classified by unanimous judgment of the panel. In addition, 11 of 17 respondents were classified as good copers by unanimous decisions. No single panel member demonstrated a strong tendency to classify the respondents either optimistically or pessimistically in comparison to the other panel members. Scudder tended to feel the respondents were a little better off than did Carlson or Williamson, while Carlson tended to take a slightly darker view than Scudder or Williamson. The results of the classification are shown in Table 11.

Table 11   Number of Classifications by Panel Members

Panel member	Good copers	Mixed copers	Poor copers
Carlson	15 (32%)	11 (23%)	21 (45%)
Scudder	17 (36%)	14 (30%)	16 (34%)
Williamson	17 (36%)	12 (26%)	18 (38%)
Aggregate	17 (36%)	12 (26%)	18 (38%)

Excerpts from Selected Interviews with Urban and Rural Relocatees and Potential Relocatees

Urban Relocatees

1. Male (Age 55)

I think that this whole JUA [dispute] was not our fault. My family had to move four times. Twice we had moved before District 6 eviction. We used to live in Oraibi. As Hopis keep moving out, they kept asking us to move. We were not reimbursed for those original homesites. . . .

We would hope that the Navajo tribe does not give up on us. We want to be part of the tribe and not be treated like we are no longer Navajos. We need services—we were given lots of promises, but we have not seen them happen. We want to know what happens to our future generation: who's going to help us when we can't make payments, when there's no food on our table? It is frightening for those of us who are getting on in years. I hope you can tell that to the people in Washington for us—also to the chairman of the Navajo tribe.

2. Female (Age 64)

Yes, I regret moving out—I should have *not* ever moved. We were told we would be moved further away from the reservation if we remained there. We got scared so [we] thought we would move nearby rather than be hauled away somewhere else. Rumors scared us. [We] also thought [they] would run out of homes for relocatees, so [we] moved here near [the] reservation. . . .

We would like to return to [the] reservation. We don't know who to turn to. Window Rock? Would they help us? We wish to have livestock again and cornfields—food. [We] always had livestock. [It's my] only livelihood—that's all I know. I wonder if I will ever have my own land again. [I] feel helpless about everything.

3. Female (Age 48)

[In town] we can't be independent anymore. We feel like prisoners here—we can't go outside, we don't know our neighbors and we can't communicate with them. At least when we lived out home we had meat from our stock, wool from our sheep, and had our own garden. We did not want to leave. But we did not want to be left behind. . . .

We worry about all our children. We wonder if they will forget to be Navajos. . . .

We are glad that you are coming to find out how we are doing—these truths must be told. We can't write and don't have the money to go to Window Rock to tell the council, but we want them to know that life is hard for us. We were given a lot of lies.

4. Male (Age 41)

All this confusion about land left me feeling so hopeless. We couldn't improve our homes, we couldn't have sheep—we were just constantly told one story after another. I moved because I got discouraged and afraid. If I waited, it might have gotten worse. . . .

A couple of times my livestock were confiscated by Hopi police, and I had to pay fines over $100. It got too difficult to keep finding money to get livestock back so I sold them all. . . .

I want to remain part of the Navajo tribe with the same rights as those on the reservation. I did not move of my free will. I still vote, and I feel that those I vote for are responsible to me. We need help too.

5. Male (Age 41)

We don't belong here—I want to go to Mexican Hat to live. My wife's family will let us live there. We plan to sell this house and buy a trailer. [According to the interviewer, when the respondent originally heard about relocation he went to a chapter meeting. A male Anglo employee came to the meeting and told them that if they didn't agree to move, someone would come in and move them anyway.]

153

6. Female (Age 36)

We relocated because it was necessary. I had to quit my job in order to move. [We came to town because of] school for [the] children. [A] homesite lease on [the] reservation is difficult to get—[we] had no choice. We would like to live on the reservation— perhaps [on my] husband's land. [According to the interviewer, the respondent's youngest boy was in a grocery shop with two other boys after school. The manager searched him, thinking he was shoplifting. She was very upset that this could happen, and she was afraid that he was selected for search because he was Indian. She sees this as discrimination. Though she would like to move to her husband's land, her relocated parents, for whom she feels responsible, would not be accepted there.]

7. Female (Age 29)

I am torn between here and home. I wish we had bought a house closer to our parents. We are all separated now. We can't get together. It all seems to cost money now. When we lived near each other money was not important. We should have waited. We should have settled closer to home. We should also have been told about how to go about buying a house and how to maintain such things as the furnace.

8. Male (Age 25)

We are happy here. But people back home say we sold out [the] Navajos and [they] even think we sold their land.

9. Female (Age 42)

QUESTION: If this relocation had not happened, would you have tried to stay on the reservation or would you have come to town anyway?

ANSWER: I would have stayed. I wonder why I left home. I should not have. Property taxes, everything costs—home insurance, utilities, maintenance costs. Being a homeowner came as a shock. I didn't know how to care for the home. I think about [my customary use area] a lot—even at night—I feel I have no land, no place to return to—"chased out" of the reservation. I had to sell all my [eleven] cattle as I was afraid they would be impounded by Hopis and cost much to get back. It's too hard living here—I am thinking about selling my home and buying a smaller house.

10. Female (Age 29)

QUESTION: Are you happy living in town or do you want to be back in Navajo country?

ANSWER: No, I am not happy and satisfied. And I do want to be back in Navajo country. I feel confined to a tiny one-half acre here.

11. Male (Age 33)

QUESTION: Are you happy living in town or do you want to be back in Navajo country?

ANSWER: We like living here [but] our hearts remain on the reservation. We'd like to obtain a homesite lease and move back.

12. Female (Over age 80)

QUESTION: How do you like living in town?

ANSWER: Not much. I had a very difficult time adjusting. I'm illiterate. I do not know directions—I get lost. This is a totally foreign place to me.

QUESTION: What is good about living in town?

ANSWER: Nothing really. I'm here only for my children's sake.

13. Male (Age 28)

I feel the NHIRC should fully counsel potential relocatees about contracts so they won't have so many problems later. Explain everything about real estate instead of taking it for granted that people know, because most likely they don't.

14. Male (Age 40)

The local welfare department says they can't assist families because of generous benefits they have received—[the] welfare department doesn't know benefits are tax exempt. We are told to contact the NHIRC for assistance in this matter.

155

15. Male (Age 60)

We moved into our house two weeks ago. We left our belongings and went back yesterday to pick them up—but found stickers all over declaring the place "U.S. Government." We couldn't get our household goods. We weren't told that they were going to replace the locks and place the stickers—we had permission to store our belongings. We weren't given any notice about the restriction. It would be appropriate if they could give some sort of notice—especially when weather prohibits us from moving as soon as we wanted to. . . .

We called the Relocation Commission, but they told us that the guy responsible was out of town. We didn't get reimbursed for our belongings.

[This family subsequently submitted a statement saying they wished "to return and live on the Navajo Reservation."]

16. Female (Age 40)

We feel that we have not gotten fair service from the real estate people. We had made a $500 deposit and when we finally bought the house, it had been rented and the house was ruined. We asked for repairs, but it was not done. Now they don't want us to come around—the Relocation Commission and the real estate people. They didn't want us to get a trailer. Maybe that would have been better.

QUESTION: Are you happy living in town or do you want to be back in Navajo country?
ANSWER: Back at home.
QUESTION: What do you miss most?
ANSWER: Our home, and [our] family living close together.

17. Male (Age 37)

QUESTION: We cannot do anything about your situation, but we can report how you feel. What do you think should be done to help you?
ANSWER: Help those who wish to stay, especially the elderly. We dearly love them so—and [we] do not want to see any tragedies, that is, forced removal. Repeal Public Law 93–531.

18. Female (Age 29)

QUESTION: Are you happy living in town or do you want to be back in Navajo country?

ANSWER: Back in Navajo country, but with my own land and home.

QUESTION: What do you miss most?

ANSWER: The big open country where we can take a backpack and start walking—just camp anywhere, ride horses, visit neighbors—where you can eat, work in the big fields with friends and relatives.

QUESTION: What do you like best in town?

ANSWER: Nothing.

19. Female (Age 31)

After a while you begin to wonder if you can go back there [to the reservation]. You just feel that you are in the middle of nowhere, actually.

20. Female (Age 28) and Male (Age 30)

WIFE: Well, it is really hard to leave the place where you were born and raised—having to sell our livestock. Now there is nothing to look forward to doing. It is like being stripped of all the things we once had. Altogether we do not like relocation. The only reason we left was for our kids—we had to make a living somehow. Another thing was my husband is a Vietnam veteran and that was not even considered. . . .

There is no place to go, since we just have a little space. Out there we could ride horses, herd sheep, let our children play in open country without having to worry about them getting in someone else's yard. There was more room to breathe out there too. Now there is nothing to do here but just sit in one place—it's like being in a jail cell.

HUSBAND: I don't like anything about living in town. There is nothing left. I'm a veteran too, and I fought in the war to help my people. Now it seems they don't consider or even appreciate that—or they would have let us stay on our land.

Rural Relocatees

21. Male (Age 49)

We do worry that during the summer when other children come home our children [will] get blamed for things other children have done—we did not have these problems before. We have gamblers [nearby] which is bad and it also invites drunks and vehicles—our children may get hurt. Our children's mental state of mind is not like it used to be before. They feel what we feel about relocation, and it frustrates them also. They quarrel more often, and they reject one another. . . .

We need a hogan to have singing ceremonies in—near this compound so we can have a traditional ceremony. I was already told by the medicine man he can't perform in a square house. We also need a farm with a big enough place to store our corn, melons, etc. We can't do it here at the compound. . . .

We are worse off now because we have to pay electricity bills and others that we did not pay before. And we had extra income from our livestock before relocation—and now we have none. . . .

My feeling is that if the Navajo tribe should ever buy out the Hopi interest I would like to move back to my former place despite the fact we already relocated.

22. Female (Age 45)

My children are not behaving right—this was not so before. Here my children don't have enough space to play. I cannot plan ahead for my children anymore. I am afraid that they will just scatter when they get older. . . .

Here my children are not stable anymore. Some of them get involved in the wrong things. . . .

I got very lonely recently. One of my children is beginning to drink a lot, and I think it is because the bars and roads are close.

23. Female (Age 34)

Yes, we do worry—because we have only one acre of land and our children have no place to live when they get older. . . .

Our house is too small. We need an addition. . . .

We were relocated without any knowledge of what we were getting into—something should be done about this kind of relocation. . . .

Our house was very cheaply built and very cold. That shouldn't happen again. . . .

I think we should be paid back for all the suffering and hardship they got us into.

24. Female (Age 42)

It seems like this is the end for us here. Our future plan for our children is disrupted. Our children were not considered in the relocation plan. . . .

We got very lonely for a while after relocation—we still do sometimes. Sometimes we ask ourselves why we relocated. We shouldn't have relocated—perhaps if we didn't relocate, our daughter would not have died.

25. Female (Age 41)

Yes, we had a hard time getting used to this place—all my children were like that, too. We think a lot about where we used to live. I even dream about it a lot—and even now, it is getting me down psychologically and physically. I get headaches often. I wish I had gone about it differently.

26. Female (Age 47)

I feel very lonely, and sometimes I dream about herding sheep—and I get sick often. I've been going to the hospital a lot. . . .

I feel like being in jail here. I live in fear—sometimes when the few sheep I have graze outside the fence I fear that one of these days a policeman will come and take me. Since we moved here it seems like we are under strict law—we are not free.

27. Male (Age 56)

We feel very bad about relocation—there is no way it is good. It's really bad. It happened with us. We lost my wife's father and mother and sister, and my daughter, too. Even if we have a home here we're still having a hard time—we have to pay to haul water and wood. When we lived in Echo Canyon we had a wagon and wagon team. And we had sheep. And

159

we had to sell them all off. We had no place to put them. They had them in a corral at the fairground and they started dying. That's why we had to sell them.

28. Female (Age 60)

At first they talked about moving us to House Rock, but I didn't want to move way off—that was why I put in my application. I wanted to be near where I had lived. They have the house up, but they haven't put in electricity. I told them we need it, and they said we couldn't afford it. It would cost $14,000 to bring electricity from White Cone Trading Post to our house. They told us to get a motor instead, but I don't want a motor. We didn't intend to move, but they made us, so I want my house to have everything. Originally, we were promised by the Relocation Commission that we would have all the facilities in the new house—water, electricity. They haven't given it to us and say the house costs too much at the present time. It's not fair—we're being forced to move. Why don't they do as they promised? They haven't even finished the basement. And they now say the sewer and water are up to the Health Service. Also they said they would have a butane tank connected to the stove and refrigerator, but they haven't done that. . . .

What is really worrying people is where to move and what kind of homes they will have. And what we ourselves worry about is having someplace for livestock—some good grazing land. We hate to move. But some have told us that if we move to the new location we can still have our homes here [on the reservation] and come back to live. But I myself understand that our place will be appraised and the value will be paid to us when we move. But some think they will get the value and still be able to come back and use the place as they like.

29. Male (Age 54)

QUESTION: What is good about relocation?
ANSWER: Nothing—unhappiness is all I know.
QUESTION: What is bad about relocation?
ANSWER: Everything. I am brokenhearted. I feel sick. I feel like I'm going to jail. We have no home, no farm, no transportation, no livestock of any kind.

30. Female (Age 40)

We are easily offended now—just because we are all depressed. I feel like my family and I have been placed out in the open with nothing to hold on to. A jail is a better place—where they care for you and feed you. . . .

Money does not give birth as sheep do—when we had sheep we had future security. If one can't work, one has sheep to support himself. Sometimes (all of a sudden) all my children get sick at the same time, and we are constantly going to Tuba City Hospital. We never used to get sick as often as we do now. When my husband got sick we ran out of money, and we were hungry. We discovered that money is not everything. When we had sheep and cattle, we could get quick cash in a case like this. . . .

I myself am very depressed. I get very weak sometimes, and I am beginning to have high blood pressure—and the doctor told me that I had a heart problem. Sometimes when we are reminded—like this questionnaire—it really gets us down again. So sometimes it is best not to be bothered—that is, being reminded about relocation. It is very depressing and hard to talk about all the suffering that our minds are going through.

[According to this woman's husband, "It is very hard for my parents because they are being pressured with two types of land disputes [Black Mesa and former JUA]. My mother is having another ceremony. Ever since the land dispute began she has had from seven to ten medicine men."]

31. Male (Age 41)

It seems like there is no place for us to move to now.

32. Female (Age 28)

[Relocation] has caused my family a divorce case—also drinking problems. [Leaving the place where one's navel cord is buried makes] a person lonely and more concerned, especially if the person has children. I worry a lot about my child, especially since we have a lot of problems with everything because we have no home at all. Winters are very hard—we sometimes have no place to go and no money to pay for rent. It really is a terrible world when there is more hardship to face. We can't make homes either [because of the freeze and the problem of getting homesite leases].

Potential Relocatees

33. Male (Over age 80)

I was raised in District 6 along with my sisters, parents, and grandfathers and grandmothers. They are all gone now—buried inside District 6. We used to live right southwest of Oraibi. I remember we were all being pushed southward all the time. . . .

We had lots of problems with the freeze, and our own children helped build this house while everyone else was getting homes built for them. We were told not to build a stronger and sturdier house because of the freeze. . . .

By burying the navel cord near the dwelling place, they tied me to the sheep so we would think about livestock [it is the same with the children]. . . .

I feel old with many children. Look at my house. I used to have many homes and many sheep and cattle. I look back at all this and now this is all I have left—and I agree with many people who do not want to move out. Listen to them carefully. I only know many old ways because I am a medicine man. I am here if our grandchildren want to learn the Navajo medicine man's way. Life is hard. We don't know how other people live. I am old and don't get around very much anymore. I [am registered] at Window Rock. I hope they look after me and know that I am here.

34. Male (Age 53) and Female (Age 38)

HUSBAND: Yes, we used to [use] our livestock in many different ways. It was our food, our money when our children needed clothing—we made rugs out of the wool, we paid our medicine man with it, and ate it during ceremonies—and we as a family were appreciated by our relatives for being generous with our food. We want to retain our livestock as much as we can. It is everything that makes us what we are today. . . .

My physical condition is fine, but since the land was partitioned this has caused me to have mental depressions that affect my physical condition—and I received some medicine from the mental health doctor that is supposed to keep my mind numb and off the subject of relocation and land dispute. . . .

We discussed relocating about eight miles southwest of Sand Springs at one time, but the people living there objected. Then we discussed moving our livestock east of Flagstaff and raising our livestock there, but there is no land for this. Everything seems hopeless, so we all decided just to remain here and not relocate—and see what they do to us.

WIFE: [The wife was weeping during this discussion.] The children's behavior has been changed. They speak of ways to solve this problem. They ask, "Why can't we just have our land back?" They worry about how we are going to live. It hurts my heart and my mind. I get so angered about it I start talking crazy—say things I should not say in Navajo. My mind is blank sometimes. . . .

This past summer [one of my children] started talking about doing something to himself. He no longer has livestock—he sold it all. He has no future for himself and no land. He has stated that he no longer cares what happens to him. He drinks all the time. His sister died recently, and the land dispute caused this. . . .

We wonder about everything. What's going to happen to us if we leave? I feel if we leave this land that we will die because we lost our home—our land that has been ours a lifetime. We worry about it when our children talk about these problems. What's going to happen to them? My latest child died recently, and I feel that somehow our child might not have wanted to live in this type of land dispute, stock reduction, etc. Maybe this is why she died. Maybe it's better—I think about this all the time. I think about how life is without livestock—I cannot imagine how it will be. . . .

Since stock reduction, we cannot have enough mutton [for the children to] have as their lunch or to take with them. We don't have any stock left to sell in case of emergencies—to buy clothing, trips to the hospital, to see our children. . . .

Sometimes we feel we do not have enough labor to do our job. We are both mentally and physically disabled. We cannot do everything ourselves. . . .

There will be lots of accusations even if I move on-

163

reservation, especially if I have even one sheep. If I move to town, my children will do something wrong, and I will get blamed because they will have a hard time adjusting. They will probably throw us out of town also. I heard some people already sold their houses in town because they could not adjust. This will probably happen to me. . . .

Relocation is no good because it will ruin our thinking. It will ruin our whole outlook on life for ourselves and our children. Life will never be as good as before. All it is is heartache, mind-thinking, and heart attacks. It will cause us to fight back, and someone will get hurt. This is what it is. . . .

They will have to throw me out. I was born and raised here. My origin is here—no place else. If this is why they harm me, then let them harm me for what I believe in. I am proud that I feel this way.

35. Female (Age 54)

I have been told by the relocation office that there is no sense to argue and have a dispute over land because this land that we occupy is federally owned. The federal government has the greatest amount of control over it and can do what it pleases with it. I am inclined to believe this because it's the federal government who seems to be doing a lot of things—that is, fencing, brush control—as it wishes. Where is *our* tribal government?

36. Male (Age 35)

This is tragic because [my wife] was born here. The livestock know where home is also. It is only natural that you have the most comfort where you've lived for a long time. In my case, this is my birthplace. . . .

We want our land given back to us. No other place—no site on this earth—will ever replace where we live now.

37. Male (Age 30)

I shall move only if they prepare where we—my mother and I—are going. I want to see it first—then I'll decide. If the relocation site is not favorable to me, no force will make me move. I also want to see who is behind all of this. . . .

I think it's up to the people who are living here on the Hopi side. I will join with the people [the majority] on what they want to do. If they want to contest it further, or relocate—I'll go [along]. Or if the majority want to fight I shall join to do that.

38. Female (Age 67)

I think there is little that can be done to resolve the land dispute. I fear there is a greater chance that we will be forced to move. The consequence of this will be the damage to the mentality of the individuals involved.

39. Female (Age 34)

[This woman, with some higher education, filled out her own interview. Her first five points relate to livestock reduction.]

1. It causes [a] breakdown in [the] family tradition—the Navajo people were made to have livestock.
2. Having livestock is like having money in the bank.
3. We will have no livestock left to pass down to children/grand-children for daily survival need [food], ceremonies—we will lose all grazing rights and all other land use rights.
4. The losing of livestock will cause our people to live in [a] community type setting as opposed to [a] rural type setting.
5. It will cause us to have mental breakdowns—our people feel they cannot live without livestock. They feel their livestock is a part of them. They lose sleep if one or two do not come home with the herd in the evening. They know each and every one of their livestock. Prayers and other ceremonies are made for the livestock as well as for the [Navajo] people.

I think the best thing anyone can do is to repeal Public Law 93–531 in its entirety. The Hopi tribe never had our interest in this matter until the federal government gave them the interest. This whole matter should be settled between the federal government and the Hopi tribe— to pay each other off for their interest. The Navajo Tribal Council needs to publicly take a position to repeal this law.

40. Female (Age 52)

[We did not get a fair appraisal for our] sweathouse that is used for ceremonial purposes as one cannot put a monetary value on it. I feel it's priceless because of its spiritual value to Navajos. I don't believe non-Navajo's [can] understand its meaning and value to us.

I would like the Navajo tribe to buy back lands for us so we would not have to move to some unknown land. I have not had peace of mind since this dispute began, especially in recent years. People also spread rumors, and it's difficult to tell what's fact anymore. We are just scaring one another that way. Some people believe everything they hear.

41. Female (Age 60)

When we used to have sheep, we used to butcher them. Now we have no fresh meat—we're hungry for it all year round. It costs too much when you buy it from the store—just for one pound. . . .

Relocation is bad—it's no good. We were born here and lived here all our lives, and now we're pushed off. How would anyone like it? . . .

We are concerned [about burial sites]. My father is buried just inside the Hopi line—and some of my relatives. What are they going to do about this now? We don't want any money for those burials, but we wonder if we could get that land where they are buried—pay the Hopis for it. . . .

Another thing we know—no Hopi will ever live out here. They live on top of the cliff and that is where they belong. So our leaders and the Hopi leaders ought to get together and pay the Hopis and keep the land.

42. Female (Age 52) and Male (Age 68)

[According to the interviewer, the only time this family will agree to have their house appraised is if they are told a house is ready for them and they like it. Otherwise, no; and if it's in town, no. If it's inside the Navajo Reservation, yes; off-reservation, no. They will stay as long as they can and will have to see and approve before they will say yes.]

WIFE: Yes, it's true children are getting into mischief now with no stock to care for. When we had livestock at home, they used to herd and have fun. Since the livestock are gone, those kids—especially with cars—go off to town maybe for two to three days. They don't care to stay home. This is what we are really worried about with our children. And our health isn't good with the way we feel. We sit and worry about our children, our home, and our livestock—and where we'll move. Nobody knows. You know the mistakes my children have made—my son in Winslow has no job or money. My husband gives some of his pension, and I have pawned jewelry to help those children in Winslow. I just feel down with the worry about it all.

HUSBAND: This is our home. We're not asking to go out—it's the law that is telling us to go out and make a living somewhere else. We think no—this is our home where we make a living on the land.

43. Female (Age 67)

QUESTION: Has relocation affected your children's behavior?

ANSWER: Yes. You can tell—they get sick from worrying. We all do that, get sick. When our tears go down, then we get headaches. When we're alone, we shed tears over it all. It's the only way we can cope with it.

I want to stay on where I was born—even if it's the Hopi side. I hate to leave that land up there—because my old people stayed up there, my father's side. I wish only they could make it Navajo land again. The Hopis didn't live anyplace there when I was born. Let them live in District 6. But we built our houses. We want to live there and have our stock again. It's not good for us to eat frozen food. It doesn't taste good to us. We weren't raised with that frozen food. They promised us so many things when they were trying to reduce the stock—they promised us lots of jobs. But now there is only CETA, and they say that it's just training. We want regular jobs. My grandchildren are educated, but they have no jobs. They promised us jobs, but the government thinks nothing about its promises. . . .

And wood—it's up the mountain where we get the wood. Now Hopis have that, and they'll refuse us [permission] to get it—and they made a fence to keep us out. We don't have electricity and coal, and it's hard to get the

167

wood. So it's very hard for us. It makes us hurt to think about it all—our hearts hurt.

44. Male (Age 57)

I worried a lot since I sold my livestock. I almost cried over the last herd I sold. It seems now as though I'm becoming real old. I had some black hair three years ago, and now I'm all white—and my eyes bother me since then. And I used to get everything I needed on credit because of the stock. . . .

There is this breaking up of children and family. It may be good for some of the younger generation to be resettled in a town where they can get a job. But these old-timers—they don't know what to do. So it's best for them to stay where they were born and raised and have their own homes. I would rather see that—they will just worry about friends and livestock and strange land. Some of them will get sick, maybe die. It's already happened out here to some people [who were] told to move to another area.

45. Male (Age 56)

At this present time we have nothing. I was raised behind cattle and sheep and mostly on horseback—and I was happy and learned how to live. Now they are gone, it hurts us. It hurts our health, and we have an unhappy life at home. . . .

From the beginning the relocation program information given was that we would have [a] house with water and electricity—and they would make [the] house large enough for us all. That's what we're waiting for. . . .

There is nothing that is good [about relocation]. There's a lot bad. The homesite lease is just a tiny place. They don't explain what we can have, but we know there will be no livestock. And we will be left sitting doing nothing—with no place to go. The place over there: no good range, no house, nothing for me.

46. Male (Age 55)

Yes, there is never a day that passes that [my children] don't talk of relocation. "What's going to happen to us?" is a comment I've heard from them regularly. . . .

168

They are worried about the future of the corn patch. And the family resides near where there is water year-round. Where are we going to find another farm like this? . . .

I have never yet heard any concrete or detailed information on the land dispute and relocation from our leaders—both local and in Window Rock. Leaders [elected] are only serving their own interest. Leaders from Window Rock are confusing us like the JUA officer from Flagstaff. They are looking out for themselves rather than us. . . .

I don't know of any good thing about relocation. The bad is—the Hopis want to destroy us. They are wanting us to suffer from poverty, hunger, sickness from relocation. They are cheapening us by ridding us from our land. . . .

I will be severely damaged. I had careful instructions to further the life that my mother gave me. "From here on the farm is going to be your mother. You'll eat from *ru* and pray with pollen" were specific instructions. Now I don't know what to think. . . .

I think this type of survey is long overdue—they should define who is in opposition. Is it the Hopis for sure or some Anglos? It is a pity no one included me in this whole process. I think when you talk about land in depth you have to include farm area and its meanings, sacred places and how they were used. . . .

We want to see the results of the survey. This has never been done to date. There were reports made, committees, attorneys, council representatives working on this—but it's become terribly confusing as to what our status is.

47. Male (Age 45)

Any good [about relocation] is doubtful. If you are forced to leave, without stock, people will criticize you wherever you go. It's hard to relocate without stock. I cannot describe the feeling we have for the land—the land is the source of life and it is just devastating if we have to move. Our ancestors always lived here. The fencing crew was Navajo, but we cursed them for helping the Hopis. And what will the Hopis do with it—they are used to living on [the mesas].

48. Male (Age 57)

I feel badly about the whole issue of moving. We are split on it. Some of my children want to stay until the end and some want to move.

49. Female (Age 58)

My children want to construct new homes near here, but they can't. The children were excited about building and living here but that's become nil now. It's impossible for me to move to a distant place from here. I can't adjust to new surroundings.

If I have to be relocated, I hope I don't have to go far. I hope my new dwelling will be more adequate. I want to be compensated fairly for what I will be leaving and for my livestock permit. My feeling is terrible because of it. I say this because I feel helpless—nowhere to restart now.

50. Male (Age 72)

My home is a part of the land I reside on; therefore I feel that the value of money is not equivalent to the value of land. In this case, I feel that the amount of money given me for my home and land will never be sufficient to me. . . .

I have nowhere to move. My neighbors would not allow me to move near them. I cannot move off the reservation because I am not familiar with off-reservation lifestyles. How can I feel but depressed? No one is happy if he is forced to move without his consent. How can I be content in a totally strange environment? I continue to be depressed and confused—with loss of hope. . . .

I can only be happy here where my navel cord is. All my relatives have been here for years, and we plan to stay. . . .

I do not like the present situation now. I was not much aware of the situation when the Public Law 93–531 was established. The grassroot people were not involved in this policy making—therefore I feel that the land that I live on was [taken away] through legislation without my involvement. That makes me feel that I did not have the opportunity to defend my land. Our sacred religious deities in the Navajo way have placed the Navajo people here. I, my family, and my immediate relatives will remain here in this land that they have set aside for us. . . .

Our sacred religious sites will remain while we move. How is one to continue their religion in a strange place? Our daily lives are woven together with the land and religion. They are all one and the same—they cannot be separated. Our life, religion, and the land are thought of together. Where I reside, there are at least six sacred places, and I pray there continuously to lead a good, harmonious life. If I move and pray in a strange place, my prayers would not be the same. My harmonious life and my mental health will become unstable. . . .

When I say I pray, I pray for my children, grandchildren, and all my livestock to be well, and I hope to continue living and praying in this manner in the future.

51. Male (Age 34)

If a person relocates, the person becomes uncomfortable, depressed, and lonely for their land. I will feel depressed, lonely, sick and will constantly think of home—and eventually I will become emotionally and psychologically sick for the land where my navel cord is.

52. Male (Age 79)

We only pray the United States Courts in the future will rule in our favor and that we will live in peace with [the] Hopi Indians like it was before.

53. Female (Age 68)

No, we will not move if told to move. This land is my breath. My mother and ancestors are buried [here] and I don't want to leave.

54. Female (Age 25)

To change the lifestyle, customs, and values of a people overnight is an injustice and very wrong. The 250,000 acres of land that the Navajos are promised should be made available before relocating people. In fact, more acres should be added—the same amount of acres that have been taken by the Hopis.

55. Female (Age 31)

Land has more value than other types of wealth. We need land for our own children and their children's children. Home is land. . . .

I would feel very sad—as if losing part of me. Right now, even talking about it or thinking about it makes me feel bad, depressed. Our family

171

doesn't talk right to each other anymore. My mother and father have different ideas, and an argument starts. Brothers and sisters are all on opposite sides. The whole family is falling apart. I do not like it. I do not want to move far away from my relatives. Our family is very close, and we help each other a lot. We very much like to have our children and children's children know each other.

56. Male (Age 74)

I am a medicine man. I feel this relocation has been with us twenty years—and I feel the people have heard enough about it, and they are not going to move.

57. Female (Age 50)

I am strongly attached to my grandfather's teaching and religious belief. It surrounds me in my daily life. I will not leave the burial sites of my teachers and fathers and fathers' fathers.

58. Female (Age 32)

The bad thing [about relocation] is that we have to leave where we were born. There's no good things about relocation.

59. Female (Age 29)

My father drank due to this [relocation]. He is now deceased. My father died saying that he never wanted relocation. I feel bad about leaving and don't want to ever think about having to leave this place. Really, I don't think the Navajo tribe has done anything about our situation.

A Multivariate Approach to Adjustment to Relocation

DAVID F. ABERLE

Five variables were chosen for their assumed relevance to the adjustment of compulsory relocatees to relocation, and hence for the judgment of adjustment that is used as an index in this study. They are age, sex, education, place of relocation, and employment. For the analysis, age and education were divided approximately into quartiles rather than by the intervals that appear in Tables 2 and 4. Relocation status was dichotomized into urban relocatees whose relocation resulted from the partition of the JUA versus relocatees kept on the reservation whose relocation resulted from various causes (see Table 1). Of course, the sex of the respondent was dichotomized. Since there were only two cases of part-time employment, the employment variable was dichotomized into unemployed or part-time employed versus full-time employed. Finally, for the reasons that appear in Appendix 2, the judgment of adjustment was divided into three groups: those with serious problems, those with mixed success, and those who were coping well.

Since all variables are ordered, Goodman and Kruskal's gamma was chosen to measure relationships (Mueller, Schuessler, and Costner 1977: 207–20). Where variables are ranked for any pair of variables, gamma measures the "percentage of guessing errors eliminated by using knowledge of a second variable to predict order" for the first (Mueller, Schuessler, and Costner 1977: 217). It is a measure of association, with a range from –1.0 to +1.0. In a 2 × 2 table, gamma is identical with Yule's Q, the coefficient of association.

The focus of the analysis was to see how best to account for the

173

variation in adjustment by reference to the other variables. The analysis was necessarily multivariate, since the associations of two variables might or might not be largely mediated by a third. Three approaches were used in the analysis: interpretation of a matrix of gamma scores, a smallest-space analysis, and a series of tables in which one variable after another was used as a control while the relationships of the remainder were examined.

Matrix of Gamma Scores

Table 12 presents the matrix of gamma scores. The first thing to note is that many of the gamma scores are substantial. A gamma score may be considered a percentage of reduced error. Thus, to take the highest gamma score, ordering of cases by education reduces error by over 80 percent in ordering by relocation status. The second point for consideration is the matrix order. If a series of variables can be ordered so that the strongest relationships between pairs of variables are found between adjacent variables in the matrix, and so along the outside diagonal of the matrix, it is often reasonable—depending on the problem at hand—to infer that nonadjacent relationships are mediated by adjacent ones, and to infer causal relationships and feedbacks between adjacent variables (see Driver 1956 for an example of this approach).

Table 12   Matrix of Gamma Scores

	1. AGE	2. EDU	3. RLC	4. ADJ	5. SEX	6. EMP
1. AGE	—					
2. EDU	−0.697	—				
3. RLC	−0.633	0.809	—			
4. ADJ	−0.482	0.655	0.750	—		
5. SEX	−0.043	0.226	0.475	0.488	—	
6. EMP	−0.422	0.560	0.622	0.393	0.379	—

Key: 1. AGE: respondent's age; 2. EDU: respondent's education; 3. RLC: respondent's relocation status; 4. ADJ: judgment of respondent's overall adjustment; 5. SEX: respondent's sex; 6. EMP: respondent's employment status.

The first five variables in the matrix can be perfectly ordered. Any effort to place the employment variable closer to the other variables with which it has a high relationship (education and especially relocation locale) disorders the matrix. It is therefore left in the sixth row for subsequent discussion, and the order of the first five variables is analyzed as follows.

The relationship between age and education is strong and negative. Older Navajos have little education. Quite simply, an older Navajo's chances for any useful amount of education were slim when he was growing up, while a younger one's were considerable. A causal relationship between date of birth and education seems warranted, whereas there is no way in which level of education can influence date of birth—though it might conceivably affect survival.

The relationship between level of education and relocation is even stronger. Most educated Navajos who have undergone relocation have gone to cities; most uneducated ones have not. Since relocation is a recent experience of the individuals concerned, one that occurred after education was terminated, once again the direction of causal relationships is evident. Education presumably affects relocation site partly by the choice of the relocatee, especially for the former JUA relocatees. That is, most educated relocatees apparently apply for relocation to town. The relationship between age and place of relocation is not so strong as that between age and education or education and relocation, just as one would expect if age is mediated by education in its relationship to relocation site. Because there are so few older educated and younger uneducated people, it is hard to make a judgment as to whether age has an effect on relocation site independent of education.

Next in sequence is the relationship of relocation site and judgment of adjustment, the second highest gamma score in the matrix. Seventy-five percent of the error in the ordering of adjustment scores is eliminated by the use of the relocation status variable. Once again, although one can imagine that people who adjust badly to one setting might decide to try another, there were almost no cases of this sort in our sample.

There may be, later on, as urban relocatees attempt to move back to the reservation or rural relocatees decide to take a chance on the city. Hence the direction of cause can be inferred: from place of relocation to quality of judged adjustment. People in rural sites have more adjustment problems than people in town. As was pointed out in the general discussion of adjustment in Chapter 5, this difference in adjustment stems not from Navajo preference for urban location but from the barren situation of rural relocatees. When it is noted that age and education are more weakly related to the judgment of adjustment than is relocation site, and that age is more weakly related than education (and education than relocation site) to the adjustment score, the case for the mediation of age and education as variables by relocation site is strengthened.

The next variable in the ordered portion of the matrix is sex of respondent. Clearly the quality of adjustment to relocation does not cause the sex of the respondent. It is reasonable to infer, on the contrary, that the sex of the respondent influences adjustment to relocation. Because that is the strongest association of sex of respondent, there is no suggestion that the relationship is mediated by the other variables. The relationship between age and sex is so weak as to be irrelevant. The relationships to education (men are more educated, but not much more) and relocation site (men are more likely than women to be in an urban setting) are both weaker than the relationship between sex of respondent and adjustment. This is quite unlike the relationships, say, of age, education, and relocation to adjustment. Hence, sex of respondent is apparently independently related to adjustment. In Chapter 5 it was suggested that women experience a special deprivation as a result of relocation: they lose the power to transmit to their children the land they control by traditional rights. (Although it is true that both men and women can acquire rights to land from their mothers, it is also true that few men exercise that claim, residing instead in their wives' customary use areas. Furthermore, if a man does acquire rights to land from his mother, it passes in time to his daughters, thus again descending mainly in the female line.) Therefore women have a special reason to regret relocation.

Employment status is more weakly related to adjustment than is any other variable. Its own strongest association is with relocation status, which is not surprising when one considers that most jobs are in towns and not on the reservation. Evidently this sixth variable does not fit in with the patterns thus far delineated. These can be dealt with as relationships in one dimension: year of birth affects education, which affects relocation site, which affects adjustment, which is affected by sex of respondent. The interpretation is based on matrix order and buttressed by what is known of Navajo culture and of relocation conditions.

Smallest-Space Analysis

With smallest-space analysis, we consider relationships in two dimensions (see Figure 4). Smallest-space analysis is based on the rank-orders of the measure of association (in this case, gamma scores) and not on their absolute size. It can be done in N dimensions; and here two dimensions suffice. The representation of the mutual relationships of the variables in terms of the rank-order of their closeness to one another involves some distortion. In this case, the distortion is minimal: the Guttman-Lingoes coefficient of alienation is 0.00115 in 36 iterations (see Lingoes 1965). To carry out the analysis, we have replaced the negative sign found in the matrix for the relationships between age and all the other variables by a positive sign. One may interpret these relationships as being between youth (instead of age) and the other variables without any distortion of data, but with a resulting pattern that is easier to grasp. The analysis fits well with what has been said so far and provides some clarification with respect to employment.

The focus of special interest is the position of the adjustment variable with respect to the rest. In terms of relative distance,

177

Figure 4   Smallest-Space Analysis: Relationship Between Six Variables in Two Dimensions. Coefficient of Alienation = 0.00115 in 36 Iterations. (See Lingoes 1965: 183–84.)

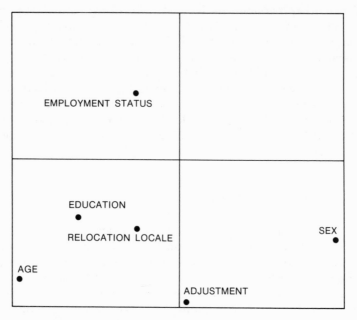

adjustment lies closest to relocation status, next closest to education, and farther from age than from either of these, which fits well with the mediation effects discussed earlier. Sex of respondent appears remote from the three variables just mentioned, which fits well with the interpretation that its effect on adjustment is independent of the others. Employment is most closely connected with relocation status—not surprisingly, since opportunities for employment vary with the rural-urban dichotomy—and is less closely connected with adjustment than is any other variable. Why this should be requires further analysis, which will be undertaken in the next section.

Control Tables

One hundred additional tables were prepared, controlling in turn for age, education, place of relocation, sex, and employment. To increase the likelihood of relatively balanced marginal frequencies, dichotomies were used wherever possible. Quartiles were collapsed for age and education, to provide median breaks. Age, employment, and relocation status were already dichotomous. The overall adjustment score was left as a trichotomy, and for this reason was not used as a control variable because the resulting frequencies were too small. The results of the analysis fit with the others.

The relationship between age and education is so strong that one cannot control for age and examine the effects of education on the subsample, or vice versa. The same is true for the relationship between rural relocation and age, education, and employment. That is, there are almost no people who were relocated to a rural setting who are young, educated, or employed. These patterns fit the prior interpretations: the relationships between age and adjustment and age and relocation status are mediated by the strong relationship between education and age. The independence of sex of respondent as a variable is shown again by the fact that it is associated with the adjustment score among young and old, educated and uneducated, and employed and unemployed. Men's adjustment is better in all these tables. Among rural relocatees, only 2 out of 13 are coping well; the rest have serious problems. Hence it is impossible to examine the relevance of other variables in accounting for the adjustment of rural relocatees. Among urban relocatees, men are better adjusted. Also among urban relocatees, adjustment varies with age and education. If sex of respondent is controlled for, the adjustment scores of men and women are influenced by age, education, and employment.

In the control tables, the reason for problems with the relationship between employment and adjustment is clarified. In the rural setting, with almost all cases having serious problems, neither employment nor any other variable can be related to adjustment. In the urban sample, although there are enough cases for analysis, the relationship of adjustment to employment is virtually lacking. Since it seemed likely that spouse's employment also played a role, a separate analysis was carried out distinguishing single and married respondents with no employment from single respondents with jobs and married respondents where either husband, wife, or both had a job. In the rural sample, with virtually no variance in adjustment, of course the new variable could not provide useful information—save that it shows that 6, rather than 3 out of 13 rural cases involved the full-time employment of the respondent, respondent's spouse, or both. In the urban sample, a gamma of 0.620 for employment of respondent, spouse, or both (versus unemployment) is found, instead of the gamma of 0.073 for employment of respondent only. Since the unit of analysis here is the adjustment of the individual respondent, and this finding uses couples as units of analysis, further exploration of the implications of this finding have been set aside for the present. The relationship indicates that it would be fruitful to use households as units, taking into account the employment and education of husband and wife, as well as the marital status of the respondents.

Analysis

In the analysis of 48 individuals who have experienced compulsory relocation, all three perspectives converge on the same interpretation of the impact of age on education, education on relocation site, and relocation site on adjustment. They suggest why the respondent's employment does not account well for adjustment and indicate that employment of one or more members of a family has a greater impact on adjustment than the respondent's employment. Many Navajos do not want to go to the city, but their rural relocation sites do not offer adequate opportunities. The old and uneducated cannot cope with the city and have difficulty surviving in the rural setting. Women experience special pain as a result of relocation, whatever their location.

Methodological Annex

DAVID F. ABERLE and THAYER SCUDDER,
with the assistance of JOSEPH JORGENSEN

Introduction

As an impact assessment, this report has been used by the Navajo tribal administration to influence public policy. It has been used in congressional hearings, and it has been used by the public media. During this exposure, the report also has been subjected to a number of criticisms, most of which fail to take into account the special problems that confront social researchers among American Indian and other populations. The purpose of this annex is to discuss some of these criticisms. These relate to: sampling (specifically, the fact that we did not use a random sample); the use of questionnaires written in English for an opportunity sample of Navajos, most of whom spoke no English; the expertise of the research team; the use of the data gathered; and the reliability of the method for dividing Navajo relocatees according to coping ability.

Random Sampling

The purpose of a random sample in sociological research is to give the researcher the ability to generalize about the universe from which it is drawn, within certain confidence estimates. In order for a random sample to serve that purpose, three conditions must be met: it must be drawn from a defined universe in such a way that each member of the population has an equal probability of being chosen; a very high percentage of those chosen for the sample must consent to be interviewed; and the units of the sample—usually individuals—must be independent of one another with respect to the characteristics under study. The results of such investigations, normally presented as correlational evidence, explain the relations among independent and dependent variables.

Not one of these conditions can be met under existing circumstances. Without a valid list of the various populations to be sampled, no adequate random sample can be drawn. There is no such list for the potential relocatees, as is evident from the fact that the Relocation Commission does not know how many potential relocatees there are. There is also no such list for the potential hosts on the Navajo side of the former JUA partition line. Lists exist, but they are not adequate. As for the relocatees, the only definitive list available to us was for District 6 relocatees. What lists exist for those relocated in connection with the Navajo Indian Irrigation Project, for those relocated in connection with the Peabody mining operations in District 4, and for those relocated by the Navajo and Hopi Indian Relocation Commission from the Hopi portion of the former JUA are protected from use by outside research agenices by the bureaucracies that control them. Thus no adequate random sampling can be drawn.

Even if a random sample, or indeed a cluster sample, could be drawn, the experience of those who have worked in the Navajo country is that refusal rates and unavailable sample members may run to 40 percent of the sample, although in one case nearly thirty years ago the failure rate was only 8 percent (Aberle 1966: 92–93; Callaway, Levy, and Henderson 1976: 7–20). The experience of Callaway et al. is of special relevance to the present case, since part of their work was done recently in the former JUA. The higher failure rates encountered by Callaway et al. in the 1970s (as compared to Aberle's for the 1950s) plausibly result from the anxiety and distrust occasioned by such contemporary problems as relocation. In sum, the failure rate for interviewing in the Navajo country is one problem that is common to all forms of sampling among these people.

More importantly, and we discuss this below, the responses to an interview are likely to be interdependent from subject to subject because of kinship ties and other factors. These factors make it likely that if random samples had any utility for survey research, a sample composed of several large kinship groups rather than individuals might be of value. But a random sample of such groups can be drawn only if we already know an enormous amount about the people—more than is known for any except a tiny fraction of the kinship units in the Navajo country. Moreover, a random sample of such units may obscure some of the relations that are most critical. Under these circumstances, if one wishes to generalize about the target population with confidence about quantities, a 100 percent sample is necessary. That is seldom feasible.

The problems of random sampling in sociological survey research among, say, the entire population of the United States are considerable. Autocorrelation is one of these problems, and it appears jointly in spatial and temporal forms. In most studies conducted on American Indian populations, random samples have even less applicability. They do not do what they are intended to do—that is, statistical independence of the units under study is not achieved. The reasons that random samples do not do what they are intended to do among American Indian populations are several, but the important point is that correlations drawn from such studies have *never* controlled for spatial and temporal autocorrelation. An Indian reservation population, because it occupies a continuous space and is connected in complex ways through ties of kinship, ceremonials, historical lifestyles, obligations, and expectations, BIA policies, federal legislation, chapter organizations, and other phenomena, is regionally and temporally intertwined. Random samples of interdependent populations in which independent variables are autocorrelated, spatially and temporally, are not valid. Autocorrelation is always based on some measure of differential

183

relatedness between pairs of cases in the sample. In the Navajo case, temporal adjacency and distance relations are both operating.

Since each measure of relatedness among pairs of cases establishes a network of relations in which traits might be autocorrelated, there is a potentially unbounded set of autocorrelation problems, one for each possible network relation. In the Navajo case, the autocorrelation problem comprises a potentially unbounded set of network relations, each of which must be examined before the possibility of autocorrelation can be discounted. In the Navajo case, time and space are "clustered" relations, yet the investigator may have little idea of what "clusterable" relations exist among the members of the population sampled. The following factors cannot be uncovered from data collected from a random sample of respondents, yet all of these must be controlled in order to obtain valid results: (1) spatial bias in interaction and communication; (2) social controls, both formal and informal, operating through clustered sociopolitical and exchange relationships; (3) constraints on access to resources through clustered relational systems; (4) relational clustering in memberships of corporate groups, religious groups, occupational groups, and social positions. These factors are recognized in most critiques of causality at the level of the "unit" of study (random samples and correlational analyses of individual, group, aggregate) in sociological and ethnological surveys.

Since random samples offer no advantages in a study such as the one undertaken here, and because a network analysis that would control for these and other variables throughout the Navajo population would require at least twenty-four man-months in order to complete, we sought an opportunity sample. In so doing, we attempted to interview all forced relocatees who were willing to talk and to express themselves in some detail. We estimate that 140 to 150 households have been forced to relocate since 1970 either because of the NIIP, the Peabody operation, or decisions regarding the former JUA. We located and interviewed members of at least one-third of those households—as samples go, that is a very large fraction. Inasmuch as random samples of interdependent populations do not allow conclusions based on data drawn from those samples to generalize to the universe, we will grant that the generalizations from our opportunity sample cannot be applied to the target population (140 to 150 households) of forced relocatees. Yet our sample sums up the responses of one-third of those households. Hence, it allows us to generalize for the 48 relocatees in our study, which includes over 50 percent of those households relocated by the Relocation Commission at the time of the study. We feel that our results, if viewed as concluding hypotheses for the remaining two-thirds of the relocated households, would prevail for the target population of 140 to 150 households.

Standardized Instruments

Our Navajo interviewers were provided with an interview schedule in English, which they translated into Navajo. For a very fine-grained study of attitudes, there would be some advantages to a standardized translation into Navajo. There are, however, two serious obstacles to developing such a standardized translation. The first is that Navajos disagree about fully adequate translations for a given question. This is not merely our experience. Professor Irvy Goossen, author of *Navajo Made Easier*, the best text for teaching Navajo, has informed David Aberle that as soon as he has developed a text using one bilingual person, another from a different region objects. Differences in personal style and local usage are sufficient to create serious disputes. The second is that Navajos fluent in Navajo and English and fully literate in English seldom know how to read Navajo; hence, the Navajo text is of no benefit. The alternative is that the interviewer or interpreter thoroughly understand the interview schedule and be able to clarify questions to respondents. That is the alternative we chose.

Quality of Interviewers and Interpreters

Three of the interviewers hold Ph.D. degrees in anthropology. Two, Professor Thayer Scudder and Professor Elizabeth Colson, have extensive first-hand experience in the study of people who have been subject to forced relocation. One, Professor David Aberle, has extensive first-hand experience in the study of Navajo Indians and has worked intensively in the former JUA. He first visited the former JUA in 1950; revisited it for two to two and a half months in the summers of 1965, 1966, and 1968; and has repeatedly revisited it for brief periods between 1968 and 1978. By normal standards, these three interviewers are qualified. Nevertheless, each must either use a Navajo interpreter or interview English-speaking Navajos. Navajo interviewers or interpreters are absolutely essential for field research among Navajos. It is often difficult to use interpreters or interviewers from outside the respondent's community. Our principal Navajo associates included: Betty B. G. Tippeconnie, a social worker with a master's degree who previously worked for the Relocation Commission and knew many of the former JUA relocatees; Jennie Joe, a registered nurse with a master's degree in public health, who is a graduate student in medical anthropology; Clark Etsitty, a B.A. in sociology, who has interpreted for Aberle in the past and collected data for him; Roy Walters, who was trained in the course of an earlier research project in the former Joint Use Area; and Kenneth Y. Begishe, a lecturer at the Shiprock campus of the Navajo Community College, who was trained by the anthropological linguist Oswald Werner, and is himself the coauthor of a study dealing with relocation in the Shiprock area. These associates, in addition to their knowledge of Navajo, are more highly qualified than typical large-scale project interviewers.

Together these five Navajos spent approximately forty days in the field, while Aberle, Colson, and Scudder between them spent approximately sixty days in the field. These eight investigators carried out or participated in the large majority of all interviews. Though assistance with interviewing was provided by three employees of the Navajo-Hopi Land Dispute Commission and by one trainee in the Navajo Nation's Paralegal Training Program, these interviewers were involved in only 28 out of 108 interviews, and in half of those cases they were accompanied during the interview by either Colson or Scudder.

Except for the urban relocatees, who were fairly accustomed to being interviewed, respondents were interviewed by people they knew or knew about. The issue of bias raised by the fact that four tribal employees were used for approximately 25 percent of the interviews seems less important than the issue of openness—that is, whether the investigators were able to set a context in which Navajos felt free to express themselves openly. It is evident from reading the interview protocols that they did. Aberle's interviews, mainly but not entirely in English, were all with people who knew him and felt free to talk to him. In this way we capitalized on his background and acquaintanceship in the former JUA.

Only the work of the Shiprock Research Center (now defunct) and the Wood, Vannette, and Andrews sociocultural assessment of the livestock reduction program in the former JUA have had Navajo interviewers of similar qualifications.

The Use of Data Gathered by an Opportunity Sample

The principal aim of the study was to discover whether there was reason to expect that substantial numbers of Navajos threatened with relocation are likely to have serious problems arising out of that relocation. The aim was not to make precise estimates about what percentage of Navajos thus threatened will have problems. A random sample would not have allowed valid estimates, even if such a sample had been drawn. Our opportunity samples of people who have been relocated for a variety of reasons, people who expect relocation, and people who expect to have relocatees move into their chapter (in each case, people who expressed themselves freely) can be treated as universes in themselves. Clearly we can speak accurately about the charac-

187

teristics of each such universe. Furthermore, we may develop concluding hypotheses about the larger universes from which the opportunity samples were drawn, and that is what we have done.

The major and minor problems discovered among urban relocatees are those that can be expected to recur. Major problems include nostalgia for the home area, sorrow for severed ties with rural kin, anxiety over the loss of a Navajo lifestyle, and deprivation because of being cut off from Navajo land and chapter participation. Minor but not trivial difficulties include employment problems, lack of contact with non-Navajo neighbors, inability to cope with the expenses of new homes and to manage the equipment found in a modern home, and so on. The distribution of responses gives grounds for hypothesizing that women in particular, separated from the rights in land that they had expected to transmit to their children, feel disturbed and disoriented by urban relocation. Like rural relocatees, the majority of these women are deeply troubled because they fear that they will not be able to pass Navajo culture on to their children.

We interviewed adults from more than 50 percent of the households that had been moved to town by the Relocation Commission. This is not a random sample nor a 100 percent sample, but it is a basis for making some statements about urban relocatees. Even if the remaining relocatees are all favorable to removal—which is implausible, though possible—we would still be forced to conclude that for many adult urban relocatees relocation is a stressful experience, and that the problems that have occurred for them will recur for new relocatees under present conditions.

For the reasons discussed in our study, reactions to rural relocation were even more negative. We must rely on common sense to assert that it is highly plausible that successive groups of poorly educated Navajos without livestock, if forced to relocate under similar conditions, will experience personal disorientation and economic catastrophe. Incidentally, if the study were biased as a result of its being commissioned by the Navajo tribe, surely it would not have included extensive negative comments on Navajo tribal policy such as those manifested by the Navajo Indian Irrigation Project relocation or the failure to monitor adequately the Black Mesa relocations.

Reactions of the majority of hosts to receiving relocatees were either hesitant or negative. Given the lack of provision for the employment or subsistence activities of such relocatees, this response is not surprising, and it is plausible that it will continue.

Inter-rater Reliability

Thayer Scudder, an expert on relocation, conducted a reliability check of the variable concerned with the ability of relocatees to cope. Two of the raters (A, B) were unfamiliar with research on coping and relocation, Navajo ethnography, and the current Navajo scene. Dr. Scudder (C) was the third. The percentage of overall agreement among the three raters was 75: A, B, = 70 percent; A, C = 75 percent; B, C = 79 percent. Within the 25 percent disagreement among the raters there was but a single instance in which all three raters disagreed. The details are provided in Appendix 2. There is no clear evidence of bias or chance operating in these ratings, although it is possible that the agreement between the ratings of the two uninformed raters was the lowest among the three sets because of their common lack of background information.

The use of well-educated raters without prior familiarity with the problems rated is not unusual in research. Though such an approach has both advantages and disadvantages, in this case A and B were probably characterized by a reverse bias. When Scudder asked them to serve as raters, both indicated that they did not consider relocation to be a particularly serious event. This initial reaction was based on their own mobility as highly educated Anglos (one of the raters had moved around the world as a member of a military family). Yet both ended up characterizing more relocatees as poor copers than did Scudder, whose previous research and familiarity with the relocation literature had led him to formulate a series of hypotheses about the multi-dimensional stress associated with the forced relocation of any rural population with strong ties to the land. Our relocation report shows that these hypotheses are no less applicable to the Navajos—indeed, they are shown to be especially applicable to the majority of Navajo women, as well as to the majority of men over the age of 40.

Conclusion

In sum, the open and frank discussion of their feelings and experiences by more than 100 Navajo adults, who make up several opportunity samples, is of value in drawing concluding hypotheses about reactions to relocation in the future and the likelihood of successful relocation and postrelocation rehabilitation. Much of the rest of the study assembles useful information about other relocation efforts in various parts of the world, about characteristics of the Navajo people (particularly those in the former JUA), and about economic and social conditions in the former JUA. Such information is normal in impact assessments.

References

Aberle, David F.
  1966   *The Peyote Religion Among the Navaho.* Chicago: Aldine.
  1981   Statement of David F. Aberle for Submission to the Senate
          Select Committee on Indian Affairs, May 20, 1981. Unpub-
          lished manuscript.
Bureau of Indian Affairs (Navajo Indian Office)
  1978   *Former Joint Use Area Needs Assessment Report,* Vol. A.
Callaway, D. G., J. E. Levy, and E. B. Henderson
  1976   *The Effects of Power Production and Strip Mining on Local Navajo
          Populations.* Lake Powell Research Project Bulletin No. 22.
          Tucson: University of Arizona.
Colson, Elizabeth
  1971   *The Social Consequences of Resettlement: The Impact of the Kariba
          Resettlement Upon the Gwembe Tonga.* Manchester: Manchester
          University Press.
Driver, Harold E.
  1956   *An Integration of Functional, Evolutionary, and Historical Theory
          by Means of Correlations.* Indiana University Publications in
          Anthropology and Linguistics, Memoir 12.
Family Service Agency (Fort Defiance, Arizona)
  1974   Evaluation of Navajo Families Evicted From District 6.
          Typescript.
Fried, Marc
  1963   Grieving for a Lost Home. In *The Urban Condition,* ed. L. J. Duhl,
          pp. 151–71. New York: Basic Books.
Gilbert, Betty Beetso
  1977   Navajo-Hopi Land Dispute: Impact of Forced Relocation on
          Navajo Families. Unpublished Master of Social Work thesis.
          Arizona State University, Tempe.
Gilbreath, K.
  1973   *Red Capitalism: An Analysis of the Navajo Economy.* Norman:
          University of Oklahoma Press.

Kammer, Jerry
1980   *The Second Long Walk: The Navajo-Hopi Land Dispute.* Albuquerque: University of New Mexico Press.

Killian, Ellen C.
1970   Effect of Geriatric Transfers on Mortality Rates. *Social Work* 2: 19–26.

Lingoes, J. C.
1965   An IBM-7090 Program for Guttman-Lingoes Smallest Space Analysis—1. *Behavioral Science* 10: 183–84.

Mueller, John H., Karl F. Schuessler, and Herbert L. Costner
1977   *Statistical Reasoning in Sociology,* third edition. Boston: Houghton Mifflin.

Navajo and Hopi Indian Relocation Commission
1978   Interim Progress Report. Flagstaff: NHIRC.
1979   *Program Update and Report: January.* Flagstaff: NHIRC.
1980   *Program Update and Report: May.* Flagstaff: NHIRC.
1981a   *Report and Plan.* Flagstaff: NHIRC.
1981b   *Program Update and Report: June.* Flagstaff: NHIRC.

Navajo Nation
1978a   *Former Joint Use Area Needs Assessment Report,* Vol. B.
1978b   *Overall Economic Development Program: Annual Progress Report.* Window Rock: Division of Economic Development.

Nie, Norman H., C. Hadlai Hull, Jean G. Jenkins, Karen Steinbrenner, and Dale H. Bent
1975   *Statistical Package for the Social Sciences,* second edition. New York: McGraw-Hill.

Reno, Philip
1978   Stripmined Land and Displaced People: Paying the Costs Left Behind in Navajo Resource Development. Unpublished manuscript.

Russell, Scott C.
1978   Return Per Man-Hour for Animal Husbandry: A Study of Seven Navajo Camps. Unpublished manuscript.

Schoepfle, G. M., K. Y. Begishe, R. T. Morgan, J. John, H. Thomas, and P. Reno; with J. Davis and B. Tso
1978   *A Study of Navajo Perception of the Impact of Environmental Changes Relating to Energy Resource Development.* Report prepared for the Environmental Protection Agency. Shiprock, New Mexico: Navajo Community College.

Schoepfle, G. M., K. Y. Begishe, R. T. Morgan, and A. Johnson; with P. Scott
    1980   *A Study of Navajo Perceptions of the Impact of Environmental Changes.* First Quarterly Report prepared for the Environmental Protection Agency. Shiprock, New Mexico: Navajo Community College.

Schoepfle, G. M., M. L. Burton, K. Y. Begishe, R. T. Morgan, F. Morgan, A. Johnson, L. Upshaw, and W. Collins; with K. Nabahe, J. John, M. Bauer, P. Scott, and P. Reno
    1981   *A Study of Navajo Perceptions of the Impact of Environmental Changes. Resulting from Energy Resources Development.* Final Report prepared for the Environmental Protection Agency. Shiprock, New Mexico: Navajo Community College.

Scudder, Thayer
    1973   The Human Ecology of Big Projects: River Basin Development and Resettlement. *Annual Review of Anthropology* 2: 45–61.
    1976   Social Impacts of Integrated River Basin Development on Local Populations. In *River Basin Development: Policies and Planning.* Proceedings of the United Nations Interregional Seminar on River Basin and Interbasin Development, 1: 45–52. Budapest, Hungary: Institute for Hydraulic Documentation and Education.

Scudder, Thayer, and Elizabeth Colson
    1981   From Welfare to Development: A Conceptual Framework for the Analysis of Dislocated People. In *Involuntary Migration and Resettlement: The Problems and Responses of Dislocated Peoples,* ed. Art Hansen and Anthony Oliver-Smith. Boulder, Colo.: Westview Press.

Tocqueville, Alexis de
    1945   *Democracy in America,* ed. Phillips Bradley. 2 vols. New York: Knopf.

Topper, Martin D.
    1979   *Mental Health Effects of Navajo Relocation in the Former Joint Use Area.* Report submitted to the Mental Health Branch, Navajo Area Office, Indian Health Service.
    1980   *Effects of PL 93–531 on Navajo Area Mental Health Patients from the Former Navajo-Hopi Joint Use Area.* Final report submitted to the Mental Health Branch, Navajo Area Office, Indian Health Service.

United States Congress

    1974   Public Law 93–531, The Navajo and Hopi Settlement Act.

    1975   Public Law 93–638, The Indian Self-Determination Act.

    1978a   *Congressional Record.* Extension of Remarks, August 9. E4464-6.

    1978b   Hearing before the U.S. Senate Select Committee on Indian Affairs (95th Cong., 2d sess.) on S.1714 Relating to the Relocation of Certain Hopi and Navajo Indians Pursuant to the Act of December 22, 1974.

    1978c   H.R. 11092, The Navajo and Hopi Amendments of 1978.

    1978d   Public Law 95–341, The American Indian Religious Freedom Act.

    1980   Public Law 96–305, The Navajo and Hopi Indian Relocation Amendments Act of 1980.

Verburg, Gary

    1981   Statement of Gary Verburg, Attorney for the Navajo Nation, for Submission to the Senate Select Committee on Indian Affairs, May 20, 1981. Unpublished manuscript.

Weissman, Myrna M., and Eugene S. Paykel

    1972   Moving. *Yale Alumni Magazine* 36 (October 1972): 16–19.

Wood, John J., and Walter M. Vannette

    1979   *A Preliminary Assessment of the Significance of Navajo Sacred Places in the Vicinity of Big Mountain, Arizona.* Report prepared for the Navajo and Hopi Indian Relocation Commission. Flagstaff: Northern Arizona University.

Wood, John J., Walter M. Vannette, and Michael J. Andrews

    1979   *A Sociocultural Assessment of the Livestock Reduction Program in the Navajo-Hopi Joint Use Area.* Report prepared for the Bureau of Indian Affairs. Flagstaff: Northern Arizona University.

Wood, John J., and Kathy M. Stemmler; with A. H. Wood, A. L. Homes, J. Roan, and S. Tsosie

    1981   *Land and Religion at Big Mountain: The Effects of the Navajo-Hopi Land Dispute on Navajo Well-being.* Report prepared on behalf of the Big Mountain Community. Flagstaff: Northern Arizona University.

Wyman, Leland Clifton

    1970   *Blessingway.* With Three Versions of the Myth Recorded and Translated from the Navajo by Berard Haile. Tucson: University of Arizona Press.

Yava, Albert

    1978   *Big Falling Snow.* New York: Crown Publishers.

Index

1 2 3 4 5 6 7 8 9 10 11 12 13 90 89 88 87 86 85 84 83 82